Rath & Strong's

Six Sigma Team Pocket Guide

Mary Federico
Renee Beaty

D0012099

McGraw-Hill

New York Chicago San Francisco Lisbon London
Madrid Mexico City Milan New Delhi San Juan
Seoul Singapore Sydney Toronto

The **McGraw·Hill** Companies

1 2 3 4 5 6 7 8 9 0 2VKP/2VKP 0 9 8 7 6 5 4 3

ISBN 0-07-141756-7

This publication is designed to provide accurate and authoritative information in regard to the subject matter covered. It is sold with the understanding that neither the author nor the publisher is engaged in rendering legal, accounting, or other professional service. If legal advice or other expert assistance is required, the services of a competent professional person should be sought.

> —*From a Declaration of Principles jointly*
> *adopted by a Committee of the American Bar*
> *Association and a Committee of Publishers*

McGraw-Hill books are available at special quantity discounts to use as premiums and sales promotions, or for use in corporate training programs. For more information, please write to the Director of Special Sales, McGraw-Hill, 2 Penn Plaza, New York, NY 10128. Or contact your local bookstore.

 This book is printed on recycled, acid-free paper containing a minimum of 50% recycled de-inked fiber.

CONTENTS

CONTENTS

INTRODUCTION:
Why Team and Influence Skills Are Required to Make Six Sigma Projects Work

O ur experience in helping companies implement Six Sigma has led us to an inescapable conclusion:

Having excellent technical skills and the best technical solution is not enough to ensure successful completion of your Six Sigma projects.

By "successful completion," we mean:

- The process owner has accepted and implemented the improvement
- The project has been through the control phase
- The project realized the anticipated financial and/or effectiveness gains
- The project was completed in a reasonable period of time, with minimum adverse effect on the team

IT'S NOT AS EASY AS IT SOUNDS.

We asked experienced Black Belts, Master Black Belts, and other Six Sigma experts to describe the non-technical issues that get in the way of successful completion of their projects. Here's what we heard:

- Getting team members to show up for meetings
- Maintaining momentum on the team and keeping the team focused
- Getting data from people
- Gaining cooperation and support from various stakeholders

- Convincing process owners to approve the change

In describing their ability to deal with these challenges, Six Sigma experts told us that they

- find these issues *more* challenging than those in the technical area (such as DMAIC or statistics)
- feel *less well-prepared* to deal with the issues

YOU CAN'T FORCE COOPERATION AND SUPPORT, AND YOU CAN'T DO THE ENTIRE PROJECT BY YOURSELF, SO WHAT *CAN* YOU DO?

You can develop skills that will help you successfully

- lead or participate in project teams
- influence others whose help you need

The checklists, worksheets, and other job aids in this *Pocket Guide* are designed to help you accomplish this. Just as you've become familiar with the DMAIC process and (if you're a Black Belt or Green Belt) the statistical tools, you should do the same with the tools in this guide. See what's available and what's appropriate, and be ready to use the right tool at the right time.

WHAT IF YOUR ORGANIZATION'S LEADERS ARE NOT DOING EVERYTHING YOU BELIEVE IS NECESSARY TO MAKE THE SIX SIGMA INITIATIVE A SUCCESS?

What senior leaders do or don't do has a huge effect on the success of Six Sigma, but you probably have little control over those leaders. This *Pocket Guide* focuses on the areas that *are* under your control. If you follow the guide's advice on making your team effective and on -dealing with your project stakeholders, you'll be maximizing your chances of success.

How to Use This *Pocket Guide*

Here are some some possible alternatives for getting started with the *Pocket Guide*:

1. If you're about to start work on a DMAIC team, refer
   to *Part 1: Getting the Six Sigma Project Team
   Started*. Begin by reading the chapters appropriate to
   your role as a team leader or member.

2. If you're in the midst of the project, consider what's
   concerning you the most. Look through the table of
   contents and job aids for topics that seem relevant,
   and read those chapters first.

3. Identify a specific problem that you're having on your
   team, and turn to the *Six Sigma Team Problem-
   Solving Grid*. See if your problem is listed under the
   DMAIC phase you're currently in, or under the "All
   Phases" section. If so, refer to the chapters identified
   as addressing that problem.

4. Start with Chapter 10 (*The "Politics" of Six Sigma
   Projects: Planning to Get Support and Cooperation
   from People Outside the Team*), and identify, analyze,
   and create a plan for your Six Sigma Project stakeholders. As you work through this planning exercise,
   read the chapters referenced in the instructions.

5. Browse through the entire guide in chapter order, so
   that you gain some familiarity with the approaches.
   Come back to the guide when you need it, for some
   "just in time" help.

Good luck with your project!

PART I

GETTING THE SIX SIGMA PROJECT TEAM STARTED

CHAPTER 1.
The Role of the Project Team Leader

The team leader (who may be a Black Belt, or someone working closely with a BB or MBB) has overall
responsibility for making sure the work of the team gets
done. Those responsibilities start before the team comes
together, and continue after the team has disbanded.

BEFORE

The team leader gets the team started. Tool 1-1 outlines
what the team leader should do to prepare for the first
meeting. For some projects, the team leader may be asked
to select or recommend members of the project team.
Tool 1-2 gives principles and guidelines for selecting team
members.

DURING

The team leader keeps the team on track, acts as the primary point of contact to the rest of the organization, and
works to gain stakeholder commitment to the project.
(Refer to Chapters 3, 4, 5, 10, and 11 for help in these
areas.)

Tools 1-3 and 1-4 give you ideas for the agenda for
the first team meeting and some icebreaking ideas to get
the meeting started.

AFTER

The team leader ensures that the team's work is docu-
mented, hands the project off to the process owner, and
debriefs the Project Sponsor/Champion.

TEAM LEADER CHECKLIST:
What to Do Before the First
Six Sigma Project Team Meeting

Draft preliminary charter with champion/sponsor. Include:

- ❏ Project description
- ❏ Scope
- ❏ Goals and measures (indicators)
- ❏ Expected business results
- ❏ Team members
- ❏ Support required
- ❏ Expected customer benefits
- ❏ Schedule

- ❏ If required, select team members (see Tool 1-2 for guidelines).
- ❏ Contact and welcome members to the team.
- ❏ Draft initial agenda for first meeting (see Tool 1-3 for sample).
- ❏ Send out preliminary charter and initial agenda for comment; incorporate suggestions prior to meeting.
- ❏ Establish team meeting logistics.
- ❏ Select an icebreaker for the meeting (see Tool 1-4 for samples).
- ❏ Establish a relationship and expectations with the process owner.
- ❏ Do a stakeholder analysis on those you've selected as team members.
- ❏ Begin to create a list of people outside the team whose support you'll need.

Tool 1-1.

TEAM LEADER GUIDELINES:
How to Select the Right Project Team Members

Key Principle

While team leaders must ensure that the work gets done, it is not their responsibility to actually *do* all the project work. The main reason for having a project team is that each member brings something important to the project, so the work can be divided among contributing members.

Guidelines

❑ Consider including a combination of people who:
   - have detailed knowledge of the target process.
   - have the technical skills required to complete the project.
   - can help build commitment and buy-in to the project and its outcomes by virtue of being involved from the start.

❑ Identify the main activities of the project and ensure that you have the right people to handle them.

❑ Look in the workgroup of the target process and ensure those closest to the work are represented.

❑ Consider support groups (HR, IT, Marketing, etc.) whose buy-in you will eventually need.

❑ Ensure Finance is involved, even if not on the core team.

❑ Include members who can represent internal and external customers and suppliers.

Tool 1-2.

SAMPLE AGENDA:
First Six Sigma
Project Team Meeting

Attendees: [list]		
Date: xx/xx/xx	**Time:** xx:xx xm - xx:xx xm	**Place:** xxxxx

Purpose of Meeting: Kickoff of [name of Six Sigma project] project team

Agenda Items:
- Welcome
- Introductions
- Discussion of team members' goals, expectations, potential contribution, desired team role, concerns, team norms, etc.
- Review of project charter
- Preliminary list of project stakeholders
- List action items related to member concerns, project charter, preparation for next meeting
- Set agenda and time for next meeting
- Evaluate meeting
- Close

Tool 1-3.

TEAM MEETING ICEBREAKERS

Famous firsts:	Ask members to share their first job, first car, first date, etc. This is an easy task that helps people who are unacquainted get to know one another.
Peak experiences:	Ask members to describe their best insight, best compliment, best work project, etc. This helps a team with a stretch goal focus on how it feels to be at the top of their form.
Birthdays:	Have participants get up and arrange themselves in order of each person's birthday. This gets people moving and talking to one another in a very non-threatening way. Alternatively, you can ask the group to do this without talking!
Question game:	Ask a question, and the first participant on your left must answer with a question, and so on, around the room. You're out if your answer isn't a question. This generally gets people laughing and breaks tension.

For additional icebreakers, see *The Big Book of Meeting Games* by Marlene Caroselli (McGraw-Hill, 2002).

Tool 1-4.

Reality Check

One Black Belt we worked with was given the task of reducing mortgage approval process time from over a month to 24 hours. She knew the task was possible because several competitors were already approving loans within 24 hours, and other divisions of her own bank were close to meeting that goal. Before the first meeting she assembled and organized all the best practices she could find.

The team she had been assigned was made up of representatives from loan processing and underwriting, so at the first meeting, she assigned implementation of each of the best practices to an appropriate team member. The team members seemed cooperative and nobody objected to their assignment, so the Black Belt was surprised that little or no progress had been made by the time the team met again, and that the pattern continued over the next few meetings.

She decided to suspend the project for one meeting and discuss why things weren't going so well. The team members were quiet at first, but soon issues began to surface. There had been no written charter for the team, so the team members weren't sure if they were supposed to help design the new process or just do what the Black Belt told them. Some of them had never even met her, and they weren't really sure what kind of power she had in the organization. All of the team members knew that the biggest delays in the approval process came because the sales force didn't always get all the documentation up front, yet there was nobody from Sales on the team. Finally, a few members admitted that they were afraid they would be eliminating their own jobs if they improved the process.

The Black Belt asked the project sponsor to step into the meeting, and together they drafted a team charter that outlined the benefits for all in improving approval time. The sponsor was able to reassure the team that there was plenty of sales volume and that, while some jobs might change, everyone would still be needed. Representatives from Sales, Customer Service, and MIS were added to the team. The team eventually reached its goal, but more than a month was lost because the team leader didn't take the time up front to use the *Team Leader Checklist: What to Do Before the First Six Sigma Project Team Meeting* and the *Sample Agenda: First Six Sigma Project Team Meeting*.

CHAPTER 2.
The Role of the Project Team Member

The team members are responsible for making sure the work of the team gets done. Those responsibilities start before the team comes together, and continue after the team has disbanded.

BEFORE

Members come to the meeting prepared. Tool 2-1 outlines what team members should do to get ready for the first meeting.

DURING

The team members participate in meetings, contribute knowledge/expertise, carry out assignments, and help gain organizational commitment to the project. (Refer to Chapters 3, 4, 5, 10, and 11 for help in these areas.)

AFTER

Members may continue to work on the process in its improved form, and may be asked to help the team leader debrief the project sponsor/champion.

Team members are selected because of the diverse skills and knowledge they bring to the task at hand. While it is important that each member clearly understands his or her role on the team, roles tend to shift and become less rigidly defined as the team progresses. The effective functioning of the team is the responsibility of *every* team member, not just the team leader or Black Belt.

TEAM MEMBER CHECKLIST:
What to Do Before the First
Six Sigma Project Team Meeting

- ❑ If you hear about a project in your area, and want to get involved, don't wait to be asked. Volunteer!
- ❑ If you've been selected to participate in a project team and you don't know why, don't wait for the first meeting to find out. Ask!
- ❑ If you haven't met the team leader, try to establish contact prior to the meeting.
- ❑ If you haven't seen a draft agenda or team charter, ask the team leader if he/she has one.
- ❑ If you have ideas for the agenda or comments on a draft, send them to the team leader prior to the first meeting.
- ❑ Discuss with your boss the project time commitments and potential conflicts with your "regular job."
- ❑ Prior to the meeting, make notes on what you might be able to contribute to the team, the role you might play, your goals and expectations relative to this project, and any concerns you may have. Be ready to share this information with the team.
- ❑ Come with an open mind and a positive attitude. This will help the team get off to a good start and make it a better experience for you and everyone else.

Tool 2-1.

Reality Check

Over lunch one day, we were listening to a friend complain that he had been asked to be part of a Six Sigma team, and that he'd had to reschedule work in order to attend the project kickoff meeting the following week. The banter was lighthearted, but it became clear that he resented being asked to take on additional work when he already had more than enough to do.

When we asked for details about the project, and why the Black Belt who was leading the team might want him to join, we learned that he didn't have any of this information. Nor did he know what kind of time commitment was involved … though he felt sure that it would be a huge inconvenience. Our suggestion, "Why don't you speak to the Black Belt and get more information?" doesn't seem like rocket science, but it honestly hadn't occurred to our friend.

The next day our friend was able to track down the Black Belt and discuss the project. He learned from the draft team charter that the team would be working on problems with the customer invoicing process.

As it turned out, our friend had an interest in ensuring that this process worked well. He supervised a group that deals directly with customer complaints … many of which involve invoice problems. Further, he had previously worked in the accounts receivable department in a company that had a nearly flawless invoicing process.

As he talked with the Black Belt, it became clear to our friend that he could play a dual role on the team: as a representative of the Voice of the Customer and as a source of ideas on invoicing best practices. He and the Black Belt also negotiated the amount of time our friend would need to commit to the team. Our friend went to his boss with a good case for off-loading some of his work. He joined the team and was able to make a significant contribution to the project's success.

If our friend had used the *Team Member Checklist: What to Do Before the First Six Sigma Project Team Meeting*, he wouldn't have waited passively for his involvement to be made clear. He would have approached the team leader to find out what was expected of him so he could carve out a role that made sense.

CHAPTER 3.
What to Do at the First Six Sigma Project Team Meeting

Key Principles

What happens at the first project team meeting sets the stage for how the team performs throughout the entire DMAIC project ... and *everyone* on the team is responsible for getting the team off to a good start.

Taking time to solicit the "Voice of the Team" before you launch into the project tasks is a good way to avoid the Six Sigma professionals' biggest first team meeting mistake (see page 18) and to achieve these important objectives:

- Identifying who on the team can (and would like to) handle different project tasks, which increases the likelihood that members will actually do those tasks.
- Aligning members' personal and business goals with the goals of the team, which makes members more likely to commit to the work of the team and therefore to show up for meetings and complete assignments.
- Reducing members' needs to restate and reestablish their credentials during subsequent team meetings, which saves meeting time.
- Giving members an opportunity to get to know each other, which builds trust, the key feature of effective teams.

TEAM LEADER CHECKLIST:
Running the First Six Sigma
Project Team Meeting

- ❏ Briefly welcome members to the meeting..
- ❏ Conduct icebreaker that allows members to learn something personal about each other and sets a relaxed tone for the meeting.
- ❏ Follow with more formal introductions and a very brief description of the project.
- ❏ Ask members to share their goals, expectations, qualifications, experience, potential role and contributions to the project, questions, and concerns. (Also share yours.) Record these on a flipchart. If people volunteer ideas for how they'd like the team to behave (i.e., its "norms"), record these also ... but do not force.
- ❏ Deal immediately with any questions, concerns, etc. members may have; record others in a "parking lot" to work on later.
- ❏ Review the project charter and strive for high-level agreement.
- ❏ Brainstorm a list of project stakeholders, i.e., those who will be affected by the project and whose commitment and support you will need (see Chapter 11). You'll work on analyzing stakeholders and planning to get their support at the next team meeting..
- ❏ List action items from this meeting, including who and when.
- ❏ Set agenda and time for next meeting.
- ❏ Ask for feedback on this meeting; thank everyone and close.

Tool 3-1. Note: This follows the draft agenda in Chapter 1, Tool 1-3, page 6.

TEAM MEMBER CHECKLIST: Participating in the First Six Sigma Project Team Meeting

❑ Participate in the icebreaker; take time to learn something personal about your fellow team members.

❑ Share your goals, expectations, qualifications, experience, potential role and contributions to the project, questions, and concerns about the project. If you have ideas for how you'd like the team to behave (i.e., its "norms"), you can mention these also ... but don't insist that everyone agree to these yet.

❑ Ensure your questions and concerns are either dealt with at the meeting or are tracked in a "parking lot" to be addressed later.

❑ Participate in the review of the project charter and give your honest opinion and ideas.

❑ Help brainstorm a list of project stakeholders, i.e., those who will be affected by the project and whose commitment and support you will need (see Chapter 11). The team will work on analyzing stakeholders and planning to get their support at the next team meeting.

❑ Volunteer for action items from this meeting as appropriate.

❑ Enter the next meeting date/time in your calendar.

❑ Give feedback on this meeting.

Tool 3-2.

Six Sigma Professionals' Biggest First Team Meeting Mistake

At the first team meeting, leaders tend to want to get to work on project tasks immediately. Sometimes team leaders who might be willing to spend time building the team are pressured by members to "get on with it." As a result, little time is spent giving members the chance to get to know each other, build trust, voice expectations/goals, establish credentials, discuss desired roles, raise concerns, etc. That approach is viewed as a waste of time instead of as a necessary warm-up step in creating a high-performance team. When the team starts to have problems later, everyone gets frustrated and things can come to a halt.

Why Does This Happen?

It's easy to see what happens when you don't accomplish task-related work at a meeting: you still have to do it and you can start to fall behind on your project schedule. It happens immediately and the connection is obvious. Since there's so much to do, and nobody wants to waste time, the need to go, go, go becomes overwhelming. Who has time for this "touchy-feely" stuff, right?

It's much harder to see what happens when you don't take the time to build the team. Sometimes the effect is not seen for a while. And most people don't recognize the connection between not spending time building a team and subsequent problems with that team, such as people not attending meetings, tasks not getting done, time wasted in pointless discussions, inability to make decisions, people behaving badly, etc.

WHAT CAN YOU DO TO AVOID THIS PROBLEM?

It's unlikely that you'll be able to do your own DOE to prove cause and effect, so take our word for it: studies have shown that time spent on teambuilding pays off in team effectiveness. Resist the temptation to push for a lot of task-related work at the first meeting. Concentrate instead on soliciting the "Voice of the Team" and establishing the foundation you'll need to successfully complete your Six Sigma project. Remember: when it comes to creating a successful team, it's "pay me now or pay me later"!

Reality Check

O ne of the best first Six Sigma team meetings we've ever seen took place at a company in serious financial trouble. The team was under tremendous pressure to take cost out of their process, and everyone was aware that some positions would be eliminated, with people redeployed to do work that was more focused on the company's current financial "fires."

The team leader used the ***Team Leader Checklist: Running the First Six Sigma Project Team Meeting***, scheduled half a day for the first meeting, and kicked it off with lunch. There was no budget, so the lunch was potluck, held in the common room of the team leader's condo. It served as a great icebreaker to just let people chat over an informal meal, away from the tension at the office. After a brief review of the team's charter, the team leader asked everyone to imagine what their work

19

lives would be like if the project were a success, and then to share their ideas with the group. Some of the responses included speculation about being laid off (a possibility) or being redeployed to other positions after the project (the most likely outcome). Talking about these potential events openly eased the tension, and a few members could even see the some positive aspects to taking on new challenges. People began to discuss their skills and experiences, in light of both the needs of the project team and the possible job changes after the project.

After discussing their own potential futures, members were able to think about how their project work would affect others in the organization. They drew up an initial draft list of those whose support they would need in order for the project to succeed and how those people might react to the project.

By the end of the meeting, the team did not have a project plan with milestones and due dates. What they *did* have was commitment from the members to the project and to each other, and the start of a stakeholder plan. They got to this point not only because the team leader used the *Team Leader Checklist*, but also because the members followed the actions suggested in the *Team Member Checklist*. Had the leader tried to force detailed project planning or had the team resisted following his lead in discussing their goals, expectations, etc., the outcome would likely have been much different.

CHAPTER 4.
How to Establish Project Team Goals, Roles, and Procedures

To be effective, the Six Sigma project teams must establish clear and agreed-upon goals, roles, and procedures.

WHAT TO DO:

The Goals, Roles, and Procedures Pyramid (page 22) tells you that to establish an effective team, you should start at the top and work your way down:

1. First, make sure everyone understands and agrees on what goal the team is trying to achieve. You already started working on this in your first team meeting, when you discussed the project charter.
2. Next, make sure that everyone on the team has a role to play in achieving the goal. You made progress in the first team meeting when team members discussed how they could contribute to the project.
3. Last, establish the procedures that will help the team do its work. Some of these may have come up in your first meeting, but you need to formalize them now.

Refer to the guidelines in Tools 4-1 to 4-4 (pages 23-26) for more detail.

GOALS, ROLES, AND PROCEDURES PYRAMID

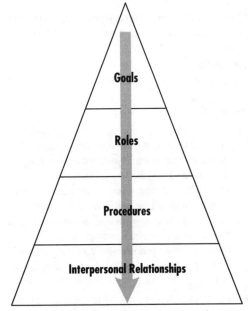

Rubin, Plovnick, and Fry, *Task-Oriented Project Development*

GUIDELINES:
Establishing Project
Team Goals

GOALS

Key Principle

If the team does not understand and agree on its goals, it cannot be effective even if the roles are clear, there are good working procedures, and team members like each other.

Guidelines

❑ *Shared vision:* Ensure all team members share the same vision of what will happen by the end of the project.

❑ *Clarity:* Make sure the team's goals are clear and unambiguous to all members.

❑ *Conflict resolution:* Identify and resolve member goals that conflict with those of the team. Such conflict can happen when members try to minimize extra work, prefer the status quo to the team's goals, view the goals as unimportant, or believe achieving the goals will have a negative impact on them.

❑ *Commitment:* Ensure team members feel they "own" the goals by involving them in goal setting.

Tool 4-1.

GUIDELINES: Establishing Project Team Roles

ROLES

Key Principle

If the roles are not clear, the team cannot be effective even if members understand and agree upon the goals, there are good working procedures, and team members like each other.

Guidelines

❑ *Clarity:* Ensure that team members accept their roles, know exactly what other members expect of them, and know what they can expect from other members.

❑ *Conflict resolution:* Identify and resolve conflicts members feel about their roles. Such conflict can happen when team members feel that it will be difficult or impossible for them to meet the team's expectations, or when they feel a conflict between their other obligations and their role on the team.

❑ *Roles to consider:* Team leader, meeting facilitator, timekeeper, scribe, recorder, and member.

Tool 4-2.

GUIDELINES:
Establishing Project
Team Procedures

PROCEDURES

Key Principle

If the team does not have good working procedures, it cannot be effective even if members understand and agree upon the goals, roles are clear, and team members like each other.

Guidelines

❑ *Meeting management:* Establish methods for preparing, conducting, and following up on project team meetings (see Chapter 5).

❑ *Conflict management:* Establish a way to deal effectively with conflicts among team members (see Chapters 7 and 8).

❑ *Decision making:* Establish the most efficient way for the team to make high-quality decisions (see Chapter 6).

❑ *DMAIC:* Ensure all members are familiar with DMAIC as the method for doing the actual work of the project (see *Rath & Strong's Six Sigma Pocket Guide*).

Tool 4-3.

GUIDELINES:
Establishing Project Team
Interpersonal Relationships

INTERPERSONAL RELATIONSHIPS

Key Principle
Interpersonal relationships are seldom the root cause of problems on the team; usually, such problems are a result of insufficient attention to goals, roles, and procedures.

Guidelines
❏ Follow guidelines above on goals, roles, and procedures.
❏ Follow the guidelines in Chapter 3 for running the first team meeting in a way that gives participants a chance to establish themselves on the team.
❏ Refer to the checklist in Chapter 8 if team members' behavior becomes a problem.

Tool 4-4.

Reality Check

At the end of the last chapter we described a project team charged with cost reductions that might result in the elimination of some jobs and creation of new jobs. The team started by imagining what the company would be like if the team were successful. The members were also asked to imagine what their own work lives would be like. It wasn't surprising that members expressed some serious conflict between the team goals and their personal goals.

They spent several hours talking about how to resolve the conflict, exploring what they might do if their current jobs were eliminated and they had to take on new responsibilities. A number of team members had spent many years in their current jobs and considered themselves experts, so it was difficult for them to imagine starting over in new positions. Eventually, all of the team members felt comfortable with the possibility and saw the team's success as their best hope of ensuring a future. A few members even got excited about the prospect of taking on new responsibilities. This is an excellent example of the team following the *Guidelines: Establishing Project Team Goals*.

The disclosure of what each member hoped to achieve as a result of the project led to some interesting discussions of the roles each would play. The team leader, whose position was not likely to change, decided to take a lower-key role and let some of the members who hoped to take on new roles be more visible with senior management.

Another member, toying with the idea of forming a training department, took on the task of designing and delivering training. The team did a good job of following the *Guidelines: Establishing Project Team Roles*.

Because the team members had disclosed so much to each other, their procedures were somewhat different from previous teams. They met off-site and agreed to a strict privacy code regarding personal information shared in the meeting. One member took minutes on a laptop during the meeting, and the team reviewed the minutes before they were shared outside the team. Finally, they agreed to use consensus to reach any decisions that might result in the elimination of jobs. The task was still difficult, but attending to the *Guidelines: Establishing Project Team Procedures* allowed the team to be successful.

PART II

TEAM SKILLS NEEDED TO
SUCCESSFULLY COMPLETE
A SIX SIGMA PROJECT

CHAPTER 5.
How to Have an Effective Project Team Meeting

Following good meeting management procedures can have a highly positive effect on your project:

- People will be more willing to attend meetings that run smoothly.
- The team will feel a sense of accomplishment that increases commitment and willingness to do project work.

WHAT TO DO:

- Take time to plan the meeting (see Tools 5-1, 5-2, 5-3).
- Follow guidelines for running an effective meeting (see Tool 5-4).
- Don't forget to follow up after the meeting (see Tool 5-5).

CHECKLIST:
Planning the Project Team Meeting

- ❏ Be clear on the meeting objective or purpose.
- ❏ Follow the worksheet in Tool 5-2 and the guidelines in Tool 5-3 to prepare an effective agenda.
- ❏ Ask for input on the agenda and make revisions as appropriate.
- ❏ Identify who should attend the meeting and whether they are available for the date you have in mind.

Provide advance notice to attendees on these meeting aspects:

- ❏ date, time, and length
- ❏ purpose
- ❏ location
- ❏ agenda
- ❏ attendees
- ❏ how to prepare/what to bring

Prepare the meeting room in advance:

- ❏ enough seating
- ❏ flipchart
- ❏ markers
- ❏ masking tape

Note: Involving attendees in planning the meeting (including setting the agenda) can increase their commitment to making the meeting work.

Tool 5-1.

SAMPLE AGENDA WORKSHEET:
Project Meeting

Attendees: [list]		
Date: xx/xx/xx	**Time:** xx:xx xm - xx:xx xm	**Place:** xxxxx

Purpose of Meeting: Kickoff of [name of Six Sigma project] project team

Agenda Items:
- Introductory remarks
- Agenda review
- Dispense with action items from last meeting
- New item A
- New item B
- Etc.
- List action items (who, what, when) from this meeting
- Set agenda and time for next meeting
- Evaluate meeting and close

Tool 5-2.

Agenda Guidelines

- ❑ Include the objective of the meeting.
- ❑ Allocate time for introductions of attendees.
- ❑ Set aside time to review and revise the agenda.
- ❑ Put agenda items in order and allocate time to items.
- ❑ Include action items from last meeting that are to be discussed at this one; list items to which team agreed and include who was responsible for each.
- ❑ Allocate time for "asides" from last meeting as appropriate.
- ❑ Include time for setting agenda and logistics for the next meeting.
- ❑ Last agenda item should be evaluating the meeting.

Tool 5-3.

CHECKLIST:
Running the Project Team Meeting

- ❑ Post the agenda on a flipchart where participants can refer to it during the meeting.
- ❑ Use a flipchart to help keep the group focused and to create a single, agreed-upon record.
- ❑ Create an "asides list" for discussion items that come up that are not on the agenda.

Dispense with each agenda item in one of these ways:

- ❑ reach a decision
- ❑ delegate item for further study
- ❑ put item on next meeting agenda
- ❑ take issue off the agenda

Keep a record of:

- ❑ key points covered
- ❑ decisions made
- ❑ action items
- ❑ persons responsible for each action item
- ❑ completion date for actions

Flipchart tips:

- ❑ use speaker's own words
- ❑ write legibly
- ❑ summarize long ideas
- ❑ number and post pages

Tool 5-4. (Continued on next page)

CHECKLIST:
Running the Project Team Meeting

Evaluate the meeting, allowing attendees to

- ❑ comment on value of the meeting
- ❑ suggest how next meeting might be improved

Tool 5-4. (Continued)

CHECKLIST:
Following up After the Project Team Meeting

Create and distribute a *short* written record that includes:

- ❑ meeting date, purpose, attendees
- ❑ key points covered
- ❑ decisions made
- ❑ action items
- ❑ persons responsible for each action item
- ❑ completion date for actions

- ❑ Identify how to incorporate participant feedback on how to improve the next meeting ... then do it

Tool 5-5.

Reality Check

Whenever we teach meeting management in the Rath & Strong "Team and Influence Skills Workshop," we feel we should apologize for telling people what they already know. Who hasn't heard that you should have an agenda? Keep a task list? Record decisions?

Then we break the class up into teams and ask them to work on a Six Sigma-related task that has relevance in their organization (for example, how to attract and retain Black Belts). Even though the teams know that they are being videotaped (for instructional purposes), and even though we have just finished discussing the need for meeting management, the teams go into their next meeting without an agenda, and no one writes anything down.

They spend the first half of the next meeting trying to remember what they agreed to at the last meeting. Usually, at least in workshops, people are willing to try using these techniques once they see how inefficient their meetings are. To our surprise, participants routinely rate this section as highly valuable. People often ask for extra copies of the *Checklist: Running the Project Team Meeting* to take to use in their Six Sigma project team meetings and their parent/ teacher organizations, condo boards, and neighborhood committees. They complain about leaving their team meetings unsure whether decisions have been made because the group is allowed to move on in the agenda (if there even is an agenda) without specifically dispensing with the current agenda item.

The simple *Checklists for Planning, Running,* and *Following up After the Project Team Meeting* described here save endless hours, but teams often resist using them. We've seen the best results when the team leader (or some other member of the team) makes a running joke out of sticking to the structure until it becomes second nature to the entire group.

CHAPTER 6.
How to Make Decisions on the Project Team

Using good decision-making procedures can have a highly positive effect on your project:

- You'll be more efficient.
- Team members will be more committed to the course of action, and thus more willing to do the project work.

WHAT TO DO:

1. Select and apply the most time-efficient decision-making approach that will also meet the needs for technical quality and acceptance (see Tool 6-1).
2. When using the group approach, choose the decision-making tools that make the most sense for the situation (see Tool 6-2).
3. Resist the temptation to overuse consensus (see Tool 6-3).

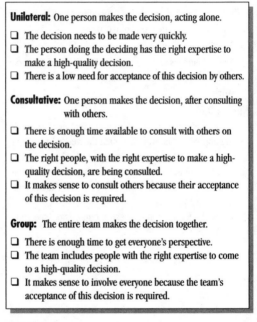

CHECKLIST:
Selecting a
Decision-Making Approach

Unilateral: One person makes the decision, acting alone.

- ❏ The decision needs to be made very quickly.
- ❏ The person doing the deciding has the right expertise to make a high-quality decision.
- ❏ There is a low need for acceptance of this decision by others.

Consultative: One person makes the decision, after consulting with others.

- ❏ There is enough time available to consult with others on the decision.
- ❏ The right people, with the right expertise to make a high-quality decision, are being consulted.
- ❏ It makes sense to consult others because their acceptance of this decision is required.

Group: The entire team makes the decision together.

- ❏ There is enough time to get everyone's perspective.
- ❏ The team includes people with the right expertise to come to a high-quality decision.
- ❏ It makes sense to involve everyone because the team's acceptance of this decision is required.

Tool 6-1.

CHECKLIST:
Selecting Group
Decision-Making Tools

Voting: The team decides through a show of hands; majority rules.

❑ The decision needs to be made quickly.

❑ The team is certain that the issue is minor enough that people are unlikely to feel resentment, and the team won't become polarized.

Polling: The team declares its opinion by a show of hands, but no decision is made.

❑ You want to find out how far the team is from agreement.

❑ You want to check for possible agreement without the risk of polarizing the team.

Multi-Voting: Each team member is allowed to vote for several ideas.

❑ You are trying to narrow down a large number of potential solutions.

❑ You are concerned about polarizing the team and want all members to feel they can win at least some of their points.

Tool 6-2. (Continued on the next page)

CHECKLIST:
Selecting Group
Decision-Making Tools

Consensus: The issue is discussed in detail, with each member getting a chance to air his/her views and try to influence others. The decision is shaped and modified to reflect different member views. Members hold out until the team reaches a decision they can support, even if it wasn't their first choice.

❑ The issue is very important.
❑ Buy-in from the entire team is required.
❑ The differing perspectives of the team members can be combined to create a better solution.
❑ There is enough time for detailed discussion and debate.

Tool 6-2. (Continued)

NOTES:
Making Project Team Decisions Through Consensus

Key Principle
Used appropriately, consensus is a decision-making approach that can result in high-quality decisions that the entire team supports and works to implement. Used inappropriately, it can be a huge waste of time and a source of frustration.

Examples of decisions for which consensus is appropriate:
- Setting the project goals
- Selecting a process improvement solution
- Picking a time for the team to meet

Examples of decisions for which consensus is inappropriate:
- Determining whether to use a t-test to analyze process data
- Deciding which production lines' data to collect
- Selecting how/where to print the project documentation report

Tips for reaching consensus:
❑ Don't just sell your idea ... ask questions.
❑ Seek ways to address concerns of all ... look for "win/win" opportunities.
❑ Search for core issues: what's important to the other person.
❑ Listen with an open mind.
❑ Try arguing the other side to ensure you really understand it.
❑ Don't allow any member to dominate.
❑ Hold out for more discussion if you don't agree.

Tool 6-3.

Reality Check

Adam, a project team leader we've known for years, is so concerned with being clear about the decision style his Six Sigma team will be using for different issues that he makes a chart. This allows the team to see which decisions he intends to make himself, which will be delegated, which will be consultative and who will be consulted, and which need to be made by the group. He uses the *Checklist: Selecting a Decision-Making Approach* with the group and records each team member's preferences for the approach to a particular decision item.

Adam started this practice after a number of difficult project meetings in which nothing seemed to be getting done. Finally, his team decided to enlighten him on why things were getting stalled, and told him that he wasn't listening to them. Adam was flabbergasted. He had always prided himself on listening carefully to the evidence presented before making a decision.

The problem was, Adam was making consultative decisions (listening to each argument, then making the decision himself) while his team thought they were making consensus decisions. (Please see *Notes: Making Project Team Decisions Through Consensus*.) As a result, the team was confused about what had been decided vs. what was still under discussion, and they began to get annoyed about what appeared to be Adam's high-handed attitude.

After giving Adam feedback on his decision-making approach, the team went through the checklists for some of their pending and recent decisions. As it turned out, a consultative style was perfectly appropriate for most of the decisions Adam was making, and the team was happy to operate that way once the decision-making strategy was clear. Adam's approach allowed the team to spend less time on less critical decisions, and reinforced the importance of allowing lots of time for those decisions for which a true consensus was needed.

CHAPTER 7.
Three Ways to Handle Project Team Conflict, and When Each Works Best

Following good conflict-management procedures can have a highly positive effect on your project:

- You'll be able to reduce the disruptive effects of interpersonal conflict, making members more willing to participate on the team.
- At the same time, you'll allow the task-related conflict that comes from productive differences of opinion—differences that can help you come up with better solutions.

WHAT TO DO:

1. Refer to Tool 7-1 and select the most appropriate approach for the conflict situation.
2. If you are dealing with an interpersonal conflict ("You don't seem to care what will happen to my department" ... "You always take her side" ... "Can't you ever shut up?"), rather than a task-related conflict (i.e., members disagree on elements of the project), you may have a problem with goals, roles, or procedures. Refer to Chapter 9 for additional guidance.
3. Resist the urge to settle for compromising when a consensus is possible and appropriate (see "Notes" on page 50).

CHECKLIST:
Conflict Management Approaches

Don't deal with it:

Knowing that not all issues are worth arguing, either ignore the conflict, postpone dealing with it, or simply agree to disagree.

- ❏ It's a non-issue: the conflict topic is not important or central enough to be worth the time.
- ❏ Tempers are too high to allow for a reasonable discussion.
- ❏ You're reasonably certain it will blow over with no adverse effects.
- ❏ Acknowledging the issue or trying to resolve it will cause more harm than good.
- ❏ There is little or no chance of coming to a satisfactory agreement.
- ❏ There's a better chance of reaching a resolution if you wait for time to pass, more info to be available, or another event to occur.

Give in:

Let the other person have his/her way.

- ❏ The issue means a lot more to the other person than it does to you.
- ❏ Team solidarity is more important than the issue itself.
- ❏ An interpersonal relationship is more important than the issue itself.
- ❏ You have no chance of prevailing.

Tool 7-1. (Continued on the next page)

CHECKLIST:
Conflict Management Approaches

- ❑ You want to show goodwill.
- ❑ You're willing to concede on this so that the other person will later return the favor on an issue that means more to you.
- ❑ It occurs to you that you could be wrong, so perhaps it's better not to push on this issue.

Hold out:

Explore issues, exchange perspectives, and strive for a solution that gives everyone some of what they want (compromise) or that fully satisfies all parties' concerns (consensus).

- ❑ The issue is important.
- ❑ Commitment to the resolution is highly important.
- ❑ You know you're right.
- ❑ Different perspectives are likely to lead to a higher-quality solution.
- ❑ The process of working through the conflict will enhance the team's understanding or performance.
- ❑ The need to resolve the issue outweighs any potential difficulties the process of resolution might cause.

Tool 7-1. (Continued)

Notes on Handling Team Conflict Through Compromising vs. Consensus-Seeking

KEY PRINCIPLE:

Seeing consensus is characterized by presenting one's own concerns, while also listening to and respecting the other person's concerns. In seeking a consensus, you are looking to solve your conflict in a way that will satisfy both parties' concerns. The more checks you have in the "Hold out" section of the *Checklist: Conflict Management Approaches*, the more likely that the issue makes it worth struggling to satisfy the concerns of both parties.

This is in contrast to compromising, in which you give up something to get something. While the result of compromising may feel fair to the parties in conflict, usually one or both parties had to give up something that they thought was important. Compromise may be the most expedient way to settle the conflict if one or more parties can check off items in the "Don't deal with it" or the "Give in" section of the *Checklist: Conflict Management Approaches*.

FOR FURTHER DETAILS:

Refer to Chapter 6 for tips on how to reach consensus when it is appropriate.

Reality Check

Six Sigma project teams often struggle with the difference between a compromise and a consensus style in dealing with conflict on the team. Compromise can usually resolve conflict fairly quickly, but when the issue is very important to the project, holding out for a consensus is worth the extra time and effort. Please see *Notes on Handling Team Conflict Through Compromising vs. Consensus-Seeking* above.

EXAMPLE OF A CONFLICT FOR WHICH CONSENSUS IS APPROPRIATE

A Six Sigma team created two processes for improving customer wait time at a bank. Each process had several proponents on the team and the debate became quite heated. The team decided to try each process in different branches and compare the results (a compromise).

Ultimately, neither process was quite right, and the team ended up taking the best elements from each (a consensus). Had the team members continued to work toward a common solution, rather than simply advocating for their own favorite, the better solution might have been reached without the time and expense of a contest.

EXAMPLE OF A CONFLICT FOR WHICH COMPROMISE IS APPROPRIATE

A Six Sigma team made up of representatives from two plants designed new touch-pad technology for collecting control chart data on production lines. The team had budget to buy touch screens for four lines. Naturally, the members from each plant wanted these first screens in their own plant, and a loud argument erupted over who deserved them more. They decided the fair thing to do was to put two of the new screens in each plant.

CHAPTER 8.
How to Deal with Difficult Project Team Members

Even on teams that are performing well, one or more members may become disruptive to the team's progress … or just make being on the team an unpleasant experience.

WHAT TO DO:

1. Refer to Chapter 9 to see if part of the problem you're having on the team is related to goals, roles, or procedures.
2. Look at the checklist in Tool 8-1 and see if you can identify the difficult team member's behavior.
3. Recognize the positive side of the behavior and build on that.
4. Try the suggested approaches for dealing with the negative aspects of the team member's behavior.
5. When you need to do something about the behavior during the team meeting, refer to Tool 8-2 for how best to proceed.

CHECKLIST:
Dealing with Difficult Team Members—
How to Recognize, What to Do

The Veteran: been there, done that

Negatives: Not open to change
Positives: Has relevant history

- ❏ Acknowledge and take advantage of experience.
- ❏ Summarize comments concisely and move on.
- ❏ Assign contributing role or responsibility.
- ❏ Call on others with differing experience.

The Idealist: everything must be perfect

Negatives: Impractical
Positives: Has vision

- ❏ Focus on common goals.
- ❏ Ask how goals can be supported.
- ❏ Ask for practical ideas.
- ❏ Ask others to build on ideas.

The Pain in the Neck: every topic involves an argument; everything is a major production

Negatives: Causes conflict, takes team off task
Positives: Plays devil's advocate

- ❏ Refer to the agenda.
- ❏ Summarize position and move on.
- ❏ Talk about how it makes the team feel.
- ❏ Offer an exchange.

Tool 8-1. (Continued on pages 55-57)

CHECKLIST:
Dealing with Difficult Team Members—
How to Recognize, What to Do

The Rambler: talks non-stop, goes on tangents

Negatives: Takes time; group loses focus

Positives: Can relieve group tension

- ❏ Acknowledge and take advantage of experience.
- ❏ Provide feedback about impact on the group.
- ❏ Interrupt.
- ❏ Avoid eye contact and call on others.

The Legalist: everything must be done exactly by the rules

Negatives: Rigid

Positives: Enforces procedures

- ❏ Enlist help.
- ❏ Ask, "What if we didn't ...?"
- ❏ Use open-ended questions.
- ❏ Use brainstorming to generate different ideas.

The Mediator: tries to resolve all team conflicts

Negatives: Can prevent productive conflict; rarely shares own ideas

Positives: Manages team conflict

- ❏ Encourage consensus.
- ❏ Ask for his/her opinion.
- ❏ Use open-ended questions.
- ❏ Set time for discussion and encourage alternate views.

Tool 8-1. (Continued)

CHECKLIST:
Dealing with Difficult Team Members—
How to Recognize, What to Do

The Power Monger: constantly trying to take over or get into position of power

Negatives: Focuses on self-promotion to detriment of team
Positives: Wants success

- ❏ Discuss effects of behavior.
- ❏ Restate and focus on goal.
- ❏ Allow others to contribute.
- ❏ Give recognition for team-oriented contributions.

The Silent Type: seldom contributes

Negatives: Group doesn't benefit from input; hard to know if committed to team decisions
Positives: Enforces procedures

- ❏ Control members who dominate.
- ❏ Ask every member to write down ideas.
- ❏ Use open-ended questions to encourage participation.
- ❏ Do a round-robin and ask each member for a contribution.

The Disengaged Member: seems to have little interest in the team's proceedings

Negatives: Creates "negative energy" in the team
Positives: Can be a reality check

- ❏ Identify possible motivators.
- ❏ Ask for suggestions.
- ❏ Acknowledge impact; don't ignore.
- ❏ Give a tangible assignment.

Tool 8-1. (Continued)

CHECKLIST:
Dealing with Difficult Team Members—
How to Recognize, What to Do

The Raging Bull: exhibits anger and hostility

Negatives: Team gets off track; personal attacks can be divisive and upsetting to members
Positives: Conflict can be productive

❑ Use conflict management approaches.
❑ Emphasize common goals.
❑ Address root cause of anger.
❑ Protect "target" members.

The Not-Enough-Time Member: never has enough time for team meetings or tasks; "has to go"

Negatives: Can drive hasty decisions or prevent team from spending time needed to get member buy-in
Positives: Can help keep team to agenda

❑ Negotiate time contract.
❑ Start and end meetings on time.
❑ Make member timekeeper.
❑ Determine if member needs help negotiating team time with his/her boss.

The Big Kahuna: operates "above" the team; too many other important things to do

Negatives: Can inhibit team; doesn't handle workload
Positives: Lends team power and stature

❑ Be realistic about potential contribution.
❑ Negotiate specific tasks.
❑ Make member part-time vs. core.
❑ Deal with his/her items first.

Tool 8-1. (Continued)

DEALING WITH DISRUPTIVE BEHAVIOR DURING THE TEAM MEETING

Start with the techniques at the top of the list—these are less confrontational. Work your way down the list as needed.

MODEL FOR DEALING with Disruptive Behavior During the Team Meeting

Ignore or avoid.

Make eye contact.

Stand up.

Walk halfway to individual.

Walk to individual and make eye contact.

Engage individual in discussion.

Allude to disruptive behavior and redirect in positive direction.

Speak to individual on a break.

Speak to individual in the meeting and involve the team.

Tool 8-2.

Reality Check

We're reminded of a team member named Debby who was part of a very vocal and opinionated Six Sigma team. Whenever the discussion began to get heated, which was often, Debby would attempt to smooth over the conflict. Debby started out being helpful, because she could usually summarize the points on each side of the argument, but her insistence on maintaining peace at any price meant that contentious issues didn't get discussed.

During one such episode, the team leader intervened, reminding the members that they had agreed to follow a consensus decision-making strategy on this particular topic, and that meant everyone's role was to hold out until they reached a solution they could all support. The group seemed clear on their goals, roles, and procedures, but as soon as voices began to be raised, Debby jumped in to smooth ruffled feathers and shut down the discussion.

The team leader used the *Checklist: Dealing with Difficult Team Members—How to Recognize, What to Do*. The Mediator seemed to apply to Debby, so the team leader made a concerted effort to get Debby to express her own opinion, rather than worrying about the tension level in the room. Debby tried, but in subsequent meetings, her efforts to shut down any sign of conflict became more and more counterproductive.

The team leader decided to use the *Model for Dealing with Disruptive Behavior During the*

Team Meeting to deal with the problem. He began by trying to catch Debby's eye, and progressed to asking her to let others finish their thoughts. Finally, he decided to talk to Debby during the next break. Debby admitted that conflict and raised voices made her terribly uncomfortable, and she just couldn't seem to stop trying to create harmony. The team leader asked Debby's permission to involve the group. They agreed that whenever anyone in the group felt the discussion was getting too heated, they could say, "Switch," and the combatants would stop and argue the opposite side. This usually got the group refocused on the issues, rather than feelings, and allowed even Debby to participate in more spirited—and productive—discussions.

CHAPTER 9.
How to Figure Out What's Wrong When the Team Isn't Working Well or Loses Momentum

It happens to most teams: at some point, the team doesn't seem to be working as well as it should. You may have a nagging suspicion that things could be more efficient ... or it may be very obvious that the work just isn't getting done. Sometimes the first thing you notice is that people aren't coming to the team meetings anymore ... or that they come, but don't seem to have any energy for the project. Perhaps the initial excitement has worn off, other priorities have been established, or frustration at the magnitude of the task has set in.

How to prevent this from happening:

1. Follow this guide's suggestions for holding the first meeting; establishing team goals, roles, and procedures; having effective meetings; making decisions; etc.

2. Take time on a regular basis to assess how the team is doing, identify any issues, and make necessary adjustments. (Think of this as the Control phase of your team, where you monitor performance to ensure it doesn't deteriorate.)

Not all problems can be prevented, however, so what should you do when you do encounter difficulties? You need to act quickly to figure out what's going on, and then do what's required to get the team back on track.

WHAT TO DO:

1. Use the Goals, Roles, and Procedures Pyramid and associated explanation (Tool 9-1) to identify the possible root cause of the team's problems.

2. If you need to pinpoint the problem more specifically, have the entire project team take the Project Team Effectiveness Survey. Look at individual scores and collective team scores to identify the areas you need to address. (See Tools 9-2 and 9-3.)

3. Follow the guidelines in Tool 9-4 for dealing with the underlying causes of the problems.

4. Look at the checklist in Tool 9-5 to ensure that you're not worrying needlessly.

5. Where possible, do this analysis and discussion as a team.

GOALS, ROLES, AND PROCEDURES PYRAMID

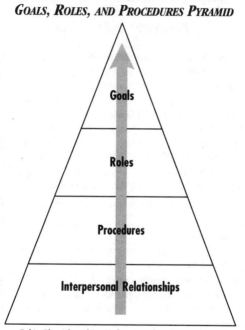

Rubin, Plovnick, and Fry, *Task-Oriented Project Development*

Note: You should look *up* one level in the pyramid to identify the root cause of a problem you're seeing at another level. For example, if you're having problems getting the team to follow procedures, the cause might be associated with unclear or conflicting roles.

USING THE GOALS, ROLES, AND PROCEDURES PYRAMID TO IDENTIFY THE CAUSE OF PROJECT TEAM PROBLEMS

Problem Area: Interpersonal Relationships

Team members seem not to be getting along. There may be arguing, accusations, conflicts, refusals to work with each other, etc.

Where to Look for Possible Cause:

Start by looking at the next higher level of the pyramid, that is, at team *procedures*. Are the right procedures in place? Have members agreed to them? Are they being enforced?

If procedures are in order, look up one more level: at member *roles*. Are they clearly defined? Agreed upon? Free of conflict?

If roles are in order, look at the team *goals*. Are they clear? Agreed upon? Free of conflict?

Problem Area: Procedures

Members aren't following procedures, or are arguing about them, or don't seem to know what they are.

Where to Look for Possible Cause:

Start by looking at the next-higher level of the pyramid: at member *roles*. Are they clearly defined? Agreed upon? Free of conflict?

If roles are in order, look at the team *goals*. Are they clear? Agreed upon? Free of conflict?

Tool 9-1. (Continued on next page)

USING THE GOALS, ROLES, AND PROCEDURES PYRAMID TO IDENTIFY THE CAUSE OF PROJECT TEAM PROBLEMS

Problem Area: Roles

Team members are not fulfilling the responsibilities of their roles, or are arguing about them, or seem to have clashing roles.

Where to Look for Possible Cause:

Start by looking at the next-higher level of the pyramid: at team *goals*. Are they clear? Agreed upon? Free of conflict?

Tool 9-1. (Continued)

PROJECT TEAM EFFECTIVENESS SURVEY

Scoring	Rarely True						True Most of the Time
	1	2	3	4	5	6	7
Goals							**Score (1-7)**
A. Shared Vision: We on the team have a clear picture of the kind of changes we want to bring about by working on this Six Sigma project. Everyone has the same image in mind.							
B. Goal Clarity: We all understand the goals and objectives of the Six Sigma project. The goals are sufficiently clear and specific to be used in setting priorities and making decisions. When questions about goals arise, we discuss and clarify them.							
C. Goal Conflict: There is agreement among us about what the goals and objectives of the project should be. If there is conflict between team goals and our business or personal goals, we explore and resolve those differences.							
D. Goal Commitment: When we set goals for our project team, or when others (such as the project champion) set realistic goals for us, we commit ourselves and pursue them vigorously. When presented with unrealistic goals, we state our position openly and try to negotiate new goals.							

Tool 9-2. (Continued on pages 67-70)

PROJECT TEAM EFFECTIVENESS SURVEY

Scoring	Rarely True						True Most of the Time
	1	2	3	4	5	6	7
Roles							**Score (1-7)**
A. Role Clarity: In every situation, we know what we and others on the team are supposed to be doing. Responsibilities are clearly defined. Whenever there is confusion, we quickly discuss and resolve the situation.							
B. Role Conflict: The roles, demands, and expectations of being on the project team are not in conflict with our non-Six Sigma project roles. In most cases, it is possible to meet the expectations of both team members and non-members.							
Procedures							
A. DMAIC: The team follows the DMAIC method for the project itself and for problems that come up on the team. We define problems carefully, identify root causes, consider alternative solutions. We are all encouraged to contribute our ideas, which are evaluated on merit. Everyone participates in problem-solving; such sessions are not dominated by one or two assertive members.							

Tool 9-2. (Continued)

PROJECT TEAM EFFECTIVENESS SURVEY

Scoring	Rarely True						True Most of the Time
	1	2	3	4	5	6	7
Procedures (Continued)							**Score (1-7)**
B. Decision Making: Decision-making methods fit the decision to be made. Team members and non-members are involved in decisions when their input is essential for a quality decision, or when their understanding and acceptance of a decision is important. The time we spend on decisions is used well rather than wasted. We make and implement necessary decisions rather than leaving them hanging.							
C. Meeting Management: Our meetings are planned and well-managed. We define and explore issues and achieve closure. We pass information efficiently and effectively. Our meetings begin and end more or less on schedule, the right people are involved, and we leave with a sense of accomplishment and time well-spent.							

Tool 9-2. (Continued)

PROJECT TEAM EFFECTIVENESS SURVEY

Scoring	Rarely True						True Most of the Time
	1	**2**	**3**	**4**	**5**	**6**	**7**
Procedures (Continued)							**Score (1-7)**
D. Conflict Management: When a disagreement arises on the team, we handle it in a manner appropriate to the conflict. Where it makes sense to smooth feelings, we do so. When it's appropriate for someone to take charge and make a decision, that happens. When compromise is called for, we all give and take a little. When the conflict is important, we ensure that the disagreeing parties present their positions in detail, we listen carefully, and we try to come to a resolution that makes sense to everyone.							
Interpersonal Relationships							
A. Support: Team members encourage each other to take responsibility for outcomes. When things aren't going well, people make an effort to help each other. We really pull together on this team.							

Tool 9-2. (Continued)

PROJECT TEAM EFFECTIVENESS SURVEY

Scoring	Rarely True						True Most of the Time
	1	2	3	4	5	6	7
Interpersonal Relationships (Continued)							**Score (1-7)**
B. Recognition: Everyone on the team recognizes that the project could not be done without the cooperation and contributions from everyone else. We are all treated as an important part of the team. When we bring up ideas or problems, people pay attention. We all have a sense that our contributions to the project are important.							
C. Trust: People on the project team trust each other to do their fair share, meet deadlines, and produce quality work.							

Tool 9-2. (Continued)

SCORING THE SURVEY:

1. For each element of team effectiveness (such as Goals), add together all team members' scores and divide by the number of team members to get an average score (1-7). Enter this information into the scoring grid in Tool 9-3.

2. Look at the variation in scores: do some team members score an item at the high end of the scale, while others score it at the low?

3. Select items for attention as directed page 72.
4. Refer to the guidelines in Tool 9-4 (page 73) for what to do.

SURVEY SCORING GRID

		Average Score
Goals	A. Shared vision	
	B. Goal clarity	
	C. Goal conflict	
	D. Goal Commitment	
Roles	A. Role Clarity	
	B. Role Conflict	
Proce-dures	A. DMAIC	
	B. Decision Making	
	C. Meeting Management	
	D. Conflict Management	
Inter-personal Relation-ships	A. Support	
	B. Recognition	
	C. Trust	

Tool 9-3.

WHERE TO FOCUS YOUR ATTENTION

Look immediately at:

• Areas with average score = 1-3

- Areas with wide variation in team member scores

Consider next:
- Areas with average score = 4-5

Address last or not at all:
- Areas with average score = 6 or above

Note that it's less important to look at the total survey score than it is to look at scores for the individual areas … both the absolute scores and the variation among team member perceptions. It is at this level that you can get at the real underlying issues—and take action that will really help.

GUIDELINES:
Dealing with Project Team Problems

If you believe the cause is ...	... then do this:
Goals	❑ Clarify, redefine, and/or renegotiate the team goals.
Roles	❑ Clarify, redefine, and/or renegotiate member roles.
Procedures	❑ Ensure team has established—and is using—procedures for running meetings, making decisions, handling conflict, etc. ❑ If existing procedures aren't working, or members don't support them, may need to get the team to define new ones. ❑ Ensure team is following DMAIC to get its project tasks accomplished.

Tool 9-4.

CHECKLIST:
Avoiding Needless Worry
About Project Team Problems

Problems	When to Worry
❑ Team can't seem to get organized around the task ❑ Members are overly polite ❑ Members telling lots of stories	Typical for a team that is just starting or one with new members. Give members time to get to know each other, establish their credentials, etc. Don't try to force task work in the first team meeting. Start worrying if this behavior continues after several meetings.
❑ Arguing, defensiveness ❑ Members ignore basic team ground rules ❑ Lots of clowning, joking, undermining authority, etc. ❑ Work not getting done	Typical for a team that is just settling in. As members get more comfortable with the team, they start to act out. It's like being a teenager. Now is the time to focus on setting goals, roles, and procedures. Start worrying if this behavior does not resolve itself within a few meetings.

Tool 9-5.

Reality Check

A Six Sigma team charged with improving first-pass yield on pharmaceutical fill lines had been working for two months. They made great progress in the first couple of weeks, but by the beginning of the third month, things began to fall apart. People started coming late for meetings, not doing their assignments, and sometimes not showing up at all. No one seemed to get along any more. The team leader, John, referred to the guidelines in *Using the Goals, Roles, and Procedures Pyramid to Identify the Cause of Project Team Problems*.

He looked at the "interpersonal relationships" problem area, because team members were not getting along. Following the guidelines, he looked up a level in the pyramid to see if the root cause of the problem might be the procedures they were following. John had to admit that they had gotten sloppy about getting the agenda out, and the task list hadn't been updated for three weeks. He resolved to do better, but got sidetracked by yet another urgent request to redo his monthly report for the upcoming board meeting. His boss told him, "Your team will just have to wait. If we don't prove to the board we can hit the numbers this quarter, they're going to close the plant." Nobody seemed to mind that John cancelled the next meeting because everybody was getting the same message from their own boss.

Eventually, John came up for air and realized that his team was weeks behind schedule. Another look at the pyramid convinced him that root cause of their difficulty was still higher than procedures. All of the team members were having difficulty with conflict between their roles on the team and their regular jobs, and the goals of the team seemed to be in conflict with the shifting goals of the company.

John decided to use the ***Project Team Effectiveness Survey*** with the team to confirm that this was what was getting in the way of their being effective. The results of the survey confirmed his suspicion. John was then able to sit with the team and the sponsor and work on clarifying and refocusing the goals of the team so that it would be clear how they could contribute to the needs of the plant. With a renewed sense of purpose, the team got back to work.

PART III

GETTING BUY-IN
FOR YOUR PROJECT

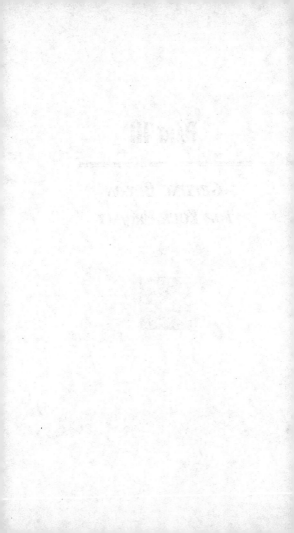

CHAPTER 10.
The "Politics" of Six Sigma Projects: Planning to Get Support and Cooperation from People Outside the Team

What would happen if, in the measure phase of DMAIC, you didn't identify the data you need, create a data-collection plan, and then implement that plan? What if you just asked random people to give you whatever data they thought might be useful? That wouldn't be an effective approach, would it?

It's no different with getting support and cooperation for your project. You can't just barrel ahead and hope for the best. The key to getting support and cooperation from people outside the team is to think in advance about what you need, and from whom ... and then plan on how to get it.

We call this approach stakeholder management, and it consists of three steps:

1. Identify your project "stakeholders."
2. Analyze them.
3. Create a plan to get their support.

Step 1. Identify Your Project Stakeholders

DEFINITION

Stakeholders are any individuals or groups who have a "stake" (or vested interest) in your project.

- They are affected by—or can affect the outcome of—your Six Sigma project.
- Either of you may lose or gain something as a result of what the other does.
- You may supply them with something they need, or vice versa.
- You can make each other's lives easier or more difficult.

WHAT TO DO:

1. Use a worksheet like that shown in Tool 10-1 to list your stakeholders. (We'll discuss the "map" later in this chapter.)
2. Use the ***Checklist: Potential Project Stakeholders*** (Tool 10-2) to identify "obvious" and "not-so-obvious" stakeholders. List them on your worksheet.
3. Think of all the major activities of your project.
   - Identify people (individuals or groups) who are affected by each activity and add them to your worksheet list.
   - Identify people who could affect the success of each activity, and add them to your list.
4. For each project stakeholder, consider whether that person's boss or direct reports are also stakeholders; add to the list as appropriate.

WORKSHEET:
Project Stakeholder Identification

Names/Titles	Map

Tool 10-1.

Note on Tool 10-2: We recommend that project teams work together on creating a project stakeholder plan to get support from those outside the team. See Chapter 1 for suggestions on how the team leader can use stakeholder planning to help the project team members feel committed to the team.

CHECKLIST:
Potential Project Stakeholders

Have you considered these obvious stakeholders?

- ❏ Project sponsor
- ❏ Project champion
- ❏ Owner of the process your project is targeting
- ❏ People who work directly on the target process
- ❏ Members of your project team (see Note, page 81)
- ❏ Your boss

Have you considered these not-so-obvious stakeholders?

- ❏ People who work indirectly on the process, or who are suppliers or customers of the process
- ❏ Those responsible for originally designing the process
- ❏ Those who have been managing the process
- ❏ The "organizational heroes" who have been fixing past or current problems on the process
- ❏ Those responsible for technology systems that support the process
- ❏ People who are back-filling for those on your project team
- ❏ Anyone who may be perceived as incapable of solving the process problem if they use outside help
- ❏ Anyone who could lose face if others find out that the process is performing poorly

---

Tool 10-2.

Step 2: Analyze Your Project Stakeholders

The more you know about your project stakeholders, the easier it is to figure out a way to get their support and cooperation. Follow this proven process to gain a clear understanding of your key stakeholders.

WHAT TO DO:

1. Narrow down your list of project stakeholders to the key players you want to analyze further. Consider including:
   - high-impact stakeholders who are potential (or known) resisters … and who might derail your project
   - high-impact stakeholders whose attitude you don't know … and who might blindside you
   - stakeholders who are potential (or known) supporters (particularly those who are high-impact, but others also) … these people can help you bring other stakeholders along

2. Use the worksheet shown in Tool 10-3 (page 86) to analyze each of your key stakeholders. An explanation of the worksheet items follows. You may want to refer to other chapters in this pocket guide for help on some of the items.

EXPLANATION OF WORKSHEET ITEMS

What I need from this stakeholder: Resources, information, permission, time, refraining from sabotage, active support, etc.

Stakeholders' interests: Tangible and intangible interests, and how they may differ from the person's stated position. (See Chapter 11 for more on interests and positions.)

How stakeholder may benefit: What the person might perceive as potential gain from project outcome/activities, or interests that could be satisfied.

How stakeholder may be hurt/inconvenienced: What the person might perceive as a potential loss or unpleasant result from the project outcome or activities … or interests that could be imperiled.

Probable response from stakeholder: Whether you think the person will be supportive, resistant, or neutral, and what you think he/she might actually do. Base your guess on what you know about reasons for resistance (see Chapter 16) and this particular person's situation.

Size of gap for this stakeholder: The gap between this person's probable response and what you need. This helps you prioritize stakeholders so that you spend your time as effectively as possible.

Key influence "levers": Key items that will help you influence this person, such as any of his/her interests that your project helps fulfill, shared values that will help smooth the way, etc.

Stakeholder's communications needs: The person's preferred way of communicating (see Chapter 12 for more on this).

Details/history of conflict with stakeholder: Any
past (or anticipated) conflicts with this person, his/her
conflict style, disruptive behavior he/she has exhibited, any
areas where your project may conflict with this person's
goal or organizational role.

Other relevant info about this stakeholder:
Anything else you know about the person that might be
helpful, including who his/her allies are, and whether you
have a relationship with any of them. (Tip: Check to see if
any of your supporters are allies of those who are resisting; they might be able to help.)

A USEFUL ADD-ON TO YOUR PROJECT STAKEHOLDER ANALYSIS

Now that you know a little more about your key stakeholders, it can be useful to return to your initial list and create
a *visual map* of the key people. A map can help you see at
a glance the status of your stakeholders: whether they are
in support of your project or not, and how much of an
impact they might have on the project (or it on them). You
can update the map as you gain more information and as
you are successful in turning people from resisters into
supporters.

WORKSHEET:
Project Stakeholder Analysis

Name of stakeholder/group:	
What I need from this stakeholder:	
Stakeholder's interests:	
How stakeholder may benefit from my project:	
How stakeholder may be hurt / inconvenienced by my project:	
Probable response from stakeholder: If resistance, why?	
How big a gap between what I need and probable response:	
Key influence "levers":	
Stakeholder's communications needs:	
Details/history of any conflicts with stakeholder (including conflict on the project team):	
Other relevant info about this stakeholder or situation:	

Tool 10-3.

Project Stakeholder Identification with Map

WHAT TO DO:

- Using a form like that shown in Tool 10-4, put words identifying your project in the middle of the map.
- Consider the degree of impact the activities of your project will have on the stakeholders and the degree of impact the stakeholders can have on the success of your project. Indicate the level of stakeholder impact (in either direction) by placing those with high impact closer to the center of the map and those with low impact farther away.
- Draw circles around stakeholders who seem likely to support your project, squares around those likely to resist, and nothing around those whose attitude you know nothing about.

Tool 10-4 is an example of a project stakeholder list with map.

HOW TO INTERPRET THE EXAMPLE

Ray, Brown, Jones, and the contractors are probable supporters, while Smith, Boyd, and the Billing Department clerks are probable resisters. The attitudes of Lee and Doe are unknown.

Jones, Boyd, Lee, Doe, and the clerks have the greatest impact on the project or the project has the greatest impact on them. Ray, Brown, Smith, and the contractors have a lower impact or are not as affected.

WORKSHEET:
Project Stakeholder Identification with Map

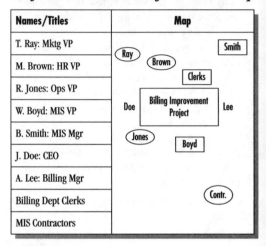

Names/Titles	Map
T. Ray: Mktg VP	
M. Brown: HR VP	
R. Jones: Ops VP	
W. Boyd: MIS VP	
B. Smith: MIS Mgr	
J. Doe: CEO	
A. Lee: Billing Mgr	
Billing Dept Clerks	
MIS Contractors	

Tool 10-4.

If these were your project stakeholders, you'd probably want to start by:

- planning to gain the support of the clerks and Boyd
- gathering more information on how Lee and Doe feel about the project
- enlisting help from supporters, starting with Jones

Step 3: Create a Project Stakeholder Plan

Having a project stakeholder plan ensures that you approach the influence part of your project with as much organization and attention as you give to the DMAIC steps. Time invested early in stakeholder planning can save you *countless* hours of dealing with resistance, redoing work, missing targets, etc.

WHAT TO DO:

1. Use the worksheet in Figure 10-5 (page 91) to create a plan for the key stakeholders you analyzed in Step 2. An explanation of the worksheet items follows. You may want to refer to other chapters in this pocket guide for help on some of the items.

2. Implement the plan, monitor progress, and update the information regularly.

EXPLANATION OF WORKSHEET ITEMS

Influence objective: Describe in detail exactly what you want the person to do, and a description of what will happen if you are successful in influencing him/her.

How to increase benefits to stakeholder: Identify anything you—or someone else with whom you have influence—can do to ensure that this person benefits from the project outcome or activities. Think of how you might change the person's perception if you perceive a benefit but he/she does not. If the person already perceives a benefit, consider how you can reinforce that perception.

How to reduce cost or inconvenience to stakeholder: Identify anything you—or someone else with whom you have influence—can do to reduce the negative effects of the project on this person. Think of how you can reframe the person's perception if he/she perceives a cost/inconvenience but you do not believe it will happen.

How to deal with conflict with stakeholder: Write down your thoughts about a good approach to resolving the conflict, given what you know about your own and this person's conflict styles (see Chapter 7 for more on conflict). If the conflict is disruptive team behavior, think of steps you might take to deal with it (see Chapter 8 for more), and consider whether you could reduce the conflict by addressing team roles or goals (see Chapters 4 and 9).

Plan for direct influence: Identify your primary and back-up influence strategies (see Chapter 11 for more information). Think of how you should communicate with this person in the course of your influence attempts (see Chapter 12).

Plan for indirect influence: If you are not the best person to do this, think about who you could ask to contact or attempt to influence this person in your place. Perhaps one of the supporters you identified earlier? Consider whether you have access to any materials, information, meetings, industry peers, etc. that might make the person more sympathetic to your project. If your stakeholder is a department or group, try to identify a friend or contact in that group who might serve as an informal link.

WORKSHEET:
Project Stakeholder Planning

Name of stakeholder/group:	
Specific influence objective:	
How to increase (or reframe) benefits to this stakeholder:	
How to reduce (or reframe) "cost" or inconvenience to this stakeholder:	
How to deal with any current or anticipated conflict with this stakeholder:	
Plan for direct influence:	
Plan for indirect influence:	
Implementation considerations (including timing and communications approach):	

Tool 10-5.

Implementation considerations: Identify the steps you'll take, when you'll take them, and whether anything else has to happen first. Determine what method of communications (face-to-face, phone, e-mail) you could and should use (see Chapters 12 through 15 for more on communicating).

Key Principles

The more broadly you think about what constitutes your universe of stakeholders, the better your plan will be. Thinking broadly allows you to minimize the chance of being blindsided by resistance from a "missed" stakeholder.

Perception is what counts; stakeholders may perceive that they will be negatively affected by a project even when that is not the case. And when considering what may be important to people, put yourself in their position and do not trivialize their concerns. (It's often said that we think people are "overreacting" whenever they react more than we would!)

You do not always have to influence people directly. The decision between a direct or indirect approach will depend on such elements as your position in the organization, the timing, your history with the person you're trying to influence, and other alternatives you may have.

If it seems too daunting to do this for all your key stakeholders, start with *one person* and see what happens.

Reality Check

It's not always easy to identify all of the stakeholders for a Six Sigma project. We once worked with a project team that identified the consolidation of all monthly reporting into a single report as an improvement. The team quickly identified the more obvious stakeholders: MIS, the administrative assistants who provided the raw data, the recipients of the report. However, as the team worked through the *Checklist: Potential Project Stakeholders*, they began to see some real issues. The administrative assistants may have delivered the raw data, but they didn't originate it. Likewise, the recipients of the various reports weren't necessarily the people who used them. It took considerable effort to find out who actually generated and used the data.

The team also found that each of the departments had its own format for reports. The team members initially assumed that the reason for this was just pride of authorship. But in the course of using the *Worksheet: Project Stakeholder Analysis*, they came to recognize that the department heads with budget authority had a very clear interest in getting credit for revenue and/or not being charged with expenses. It was this interest that drove the departments to customize reports into forms that would help them do this in a quick and easy way. Had they not recognized this concern, the team would have been focused on ways of getting the department heads to give up their pride of authorship. Instead, they identified on their

Worksheet: Project Stakeholder Planning the need to ensure that these stakeholders were still able to monitor revenue and expenses.

Early on, the team had identified the CFO, the team sponsor, as a strong supporter of the project. However, as the project progressed, it became apparent that there were serious problems with how the numbers were rolled up from the different reports and that revenue was significantly overstated. The CFO might be embarrassed or worse by the team's discovery, so they needed to reevaluate the strength of support they could expect from the CFO. Had the team simply forged ahead, it was highly likely that the CFO would not have continued to support them ... and they would have been blindsided by what appeared to be a change of heart. But by revisiting the various worksheets, the team was able to identify a potential change in this stakeholder's level of support and to adjust their approach accordingly.

CHAPTER 11.
Five Ways to Influence People to Cooperate with Your Six Sigma Project

As you work to complete your Six Sigma project, you will have to influence many people in order to get cooperation for your project, and the same approach doesn't work with everyone. So you'll need to be familiar with a variety of influence approaches (or strategies) and know how to choose among them.

DEFINITION:

Influence refers to the use of personal energy to create an impact upon, redirect, or change the outcome of a particular situation.

KEY PRINCIPLE:

Influence strategies fall on a continuum (see below), with one end being those that *push* people into action and the other being those that *pull* them (i.e., create a situation in which people *want* to do something).

What makes one influence strategy more appropriate than another is a combination of:

- the situation
- you and your capacity to influence
- the person you're trying to influence

WHAT TO DO:

1. Read through the *Checklist: Influence Strategies* (Tool 11-1) items, considering whether they apply to your situation. Put a check next to those that do.

2. Analyze your responses:
   - Look at the strategies with the most checks.
   - Consider whether all checks are equal, or whether some items have more weight in this situation; if some deserve more weight, assign additional checks to them.
   - Rank-order the strategies based on checks (adjusted for weight) and your own judgment (does the strategy seem to make sense?).

3. Use this ranking as a guideline for helping you select the appropriate influence strategy for this person.

CHECKLIST:
Influence Strategies

Telling:
- ❑ I have authority over the person—either directly or through a sponsor—and can simply tell them to do something.
- ❑ I believe that the person is willing to comply.
- ❑ I can ensure the person complies.
- ❑ I have thought through the possible short-term and long-term repercussions of this approach and still believe it is appropriate.
- ❑ The person perceives the topic as a non-issue and will not take offense.

Persuading:
- ❑ I have information the person does not have.
- ❑ The information I have is persuasive, and I'm confident that I can present it in a persuasive fashion (see Tool 11-2).
- ❑ I have enough expertise or credibility that the person will believe this information if it comes from me.
- ❑ The person is open-minded and objective with respect to this issue in general.
- ❑ The person is open-minded and objective with respect to hearing about this issue from *me*.
- ❑ I'm sure that I'm not using this approach simply because I feel comfortable with facts/data/logic (see page 101 for "Six Sigma Professionals' Biggest Influencing Mistake").

Tool 11-1. (Continued on pages 96–97)

CHECKLIST:
Influence Strategies

Negotiating:

❑ The other person and I both believe that we can each satisfy our interests better by working out an arrangement than either of us could by acting alone.

❑ I have things of value to the other person that I am willing to exchange for what I need.

❑ I believe the person shares the perception that I have something useful to exchange.

❑ I feel confident that I have identified the person's primary interests regarding this issue (see Tool 11-3).

❑ I feel comfortable negotiating with the person regardless of his/her style or position on the issue.

❑ I trust the person to honor both the letter and the spirit of any agreement.

Involving:

❑ I am sincerely willing to let the person participate in, and have some influence over, the project.

❑ The person has information, knowledge, or skills that will improve the quality of the project.

❑ This is the right time to involve the person; it will not be seen as "too little, too late."

❑ I can accommodate the extra time it will take to involve the person.

Tool 11-1. (Continued)

CHECKLIST:
Influence Strategies

Involving (Continued):
- ❏ The person has reasons to believe that his/her involvement will make a difference and lead to a positive outcome for him/her.
- ❏ The person wants to work with me.
- ❏ I have thought through whether involving this person is likely to slight others, and I have a way of dealing with such a contingency.

Appealing:
- ❏ The change I am seeking is related to a vision, values, or set of principles that the other person and I share.
- ❏ The person respects me as someone who does the right thing even when there is a personal cost associated with doing so.
- ❏ I am confident that I can truthfully and cogently communicate this message to the person.
- ❏ We share the same vision/values/principles/goals, and this project is part of an effort to further those.
- ❏ An appeal from me carries weight with this person.
- ❏ I recognize that what I'm requesting involves a sacrifice, and I respect (and share) the other person's willingness to sacrifice for the good of the organization as a whole.

Tool 11-1. (Continued)

CHECKLIST:
Is Your Data Persuasive?

- ❏ **Relevant:** You're presenting data that the person cares about and can do something about.
- ❏ **User-Friendly:** You're presenting the data in multiple forms, with pictures where possible, in language that is familiar to the person
- ❏ **Easily Verified:** You're letting the person know where the data came from, and how/by whom it was collected. (Still better: the person was involved in the collection process.)
- ❏ **Selective:** So that the person will not be overwhelmed, you've resisted the urge to include every bit of data you have, but you've prepared backup info in case it's necessary.
- ❏ **In Context:** You've made it clear to the person how this data fits in what he/she already knows, and have provided points of comparison where available and appropriate.

adapted from David Nadler, *Feedback and Organization Development: Using Data-Based Methods*

Tool 11-2.

Six Sigma Professionals' Biggest Influencing Mistake

When it's time to influence people, Six Sigma professionals tend to reach for the same strategy every time: persuasion. In many cases, this is a good approach and it works quite well. But Six Sigma professionals often do this even when the other person already has the data, or has already taken it into consideration, or is not open to hearing it. In these situations, persuasion simply doesn't work.

WHY DOES THIS HAPPEN?

People tend to use influence approaches that seem logical to them and have worked well in the past. As someone with experience in Six Sigma and its focus on data-based decisions, you can easily draw the conclusion that using data is *the* best way to influence someone. When it doesn't work, you may think it's because you don't have enough data, so you look for more and try again … and again.…

WHAT CAN YOU DO TO AVOID THIS TENDENCY?

Recognize that people consider *many* factors as they make decisions, and you often have to move beyond the data—even though this may seem like a betrayal of Six Sigma principles! Become familiar with the five influence strategies and when they are appropriate. Use the checklist to pick an approach. Try out the other strategies and see what happens. Don't let your preferred style get in the way of doing what will work best with *this person* in *this situation*.

More on Negotiating

You can negotiate effectively only if you can identify your own interests and those of the person whose cooperation you need. Sounds simple, but a common mistake is to confuse *interests* with *positions*.

Interests are things a person cares about—any concerns about the issue, any underlying wants. These can be tangible (such as money or resources) or intangible (such as power or reputation). See Tool 11-3 for hints on how to identify your project stakeholders' interests.

A *position*, on the other hand, is where a person stands on an issue. Examples:

- You want a line worker's help in collecting error rate data. The plant manager's *position* may be that no resources are available. The manager's *interest* might be that he wants to maintain control or be seen as competent (but thinks this won't happen if he gives you access to the data).

- You want a team member to attend more project meetings. Her *position* might be that she doesn't have the time. Her *interest* might be that she wants to get credit or be associated only with a success (and she's not sure if this project will succeed or whether she'll get any credit if it does).

CHECKLIST:
Identifying Your Project
Stakeholders' Interests

Have you taken these steps?

❑ Where it makes sense, you've simply asked the other person. (Note: this sends a positive signal: i.e., that you view the person's interests as important.)

❑ You've checked with others who know this person better or are in a better position to ask about interests.

❑ You've made inferences about what matters to the person based on his/her position, department goals, public behavior or comments, etc.

❑ You've imagined yourself in the other person's position and have made a list of what would be important to you if you were that person.

Have you considered these possible interests?

❑ Desire to keep job	❑ Power
❑ Money	❑ Control over events or
❑ Resources	department
❑ Need to be seen as	❑ Fairness
competent	❑ Saving face
❑ Need to prove value to the	❑ Concerns about a
organization	relationship
❑ Reputation	❑ Setting a precedent
❑ Others' perceptions	

Tool 11-3.

WHAT TO DO WHEN YOU'RE NEGOTIATING

1. Identify the issue: what you're negotiating about.
2. Identify your own and the other person's interests (see Tool 11-3 for guidance).
3. Focus on interests rather than positions. Think about what you have to offer the other person (i.e., how you might satisfy his/her interests), and how to make your offer attractive to this person. Think about what he or she has that would satisfy your interests; don't be afraid to ask for what you want or suggest trades.
4. If the other person's style bothers you, don't let it get in the way of negotiating. The goal is to get both parties' interests satisfied, not to become best friends.
5. Generate alternatives, discuss them, evaluate, select, and implement.
6. Repeat as necessary!

Reality Check

In the last chapter we described a team that identified the need to consolidate all monthly reporting into a single report. During the course of the project, the team discovered that different departments were taking credit for the same revenue, resulting in the CFO significantly overstating company earnings. While the CFO's position relative to the team didn't change from the beginning to the end of the project—he still openly supported it—his interests naturally shifted.

The team used the ***Checklist: Identifying Your Project Stakeholders' Interests*** to help them identify what the CFO's underlying interests might be. His original interests were to reduce both the time and effort required to analyze the monthly reports, and the potential for error that resulted from having different reports for each department. As the team progressed, and their analysis uncovered the unexpected issue of overstated earnings, the CFO's interests shifted to not being seen as responsible for the overstatement and, finally, to keeping his job. After reviewing what they knew about the CFO and having a confidential discussion with the Master Black Belt (a long-time colleague to the CFO), the team concluded that the CFO's need to be seen as competent and valuable to the organization was a stronger interest than his need to save face.

The team then used the ***Checklist: Influence Strategies*** to identify an appropriate strategy for getting the CFO's support. They decided on a strategy of asking for much more direct involvement of the CFO in uncovering the extent of the problem and communicating the issues and solutions to the organization. The CFO responded to the team's request, and the project was able to continue.

CHAPTER 12.
How to Communicate with People Whose Help You Need

If you want to get support and cooperation for your Six Sigma project, you need to know how to communicate about the project and your needs. The key is to talk to the people whose help you need in the way that is most appealing to *them*, not necessarily what is most comfortable for *you*. To do this, you need to figure out how they prefer to communicate, then adapt your style to theirs.

WHAT TO DO:

1. Pick people whose help you need, and consider what you know about them, including the way they communicate, how they act, the positions they have in the organization.

2. Use the checklist in Tool 12-1 to help you figure out how you should communicate with each person selected, based on what you know about each of them.

3. Use the checklist in Tool 12-2 to ensure that you don't make the fundamental mistake of using the wrong communication medium.

Figuring out how someone likes to communicate and then adjusting to that person takes you out of your comfort zone and may feel odd at first. But you'll find that when you learn to do it well, this approach can drastically increase your ability to get cooperation and support.

As you review Tool 12-1 (pages 109-111), note that the audience groups are not mutually exclusive. A person might interrupt people *and* tell stories *and* ask a lot of questions. But these behaviors often cluster together. Just try to get a general sense of the person.

CHECKLIST:
Matching Your Communication to the Person Whose Help You Need

If You Know the Person ...	You Should ...
Audience Group 1 ❑ Talks fast. ❑ Interrupts. ❑ Finishes others' sentences. ❑ Cuts people off. ❑ Hurries the speaker. ❑ Reads ahead. ❑ Acts impatient. ❑ Looks at watch/ clock. ❑ Is over-scheduled. ❑ Leaves/ends meetings early. ❑ Asks for an action plan with schedule. ❑ Has little appetite for detail. ❑ Has very senior management position.	❑ Check at start: amount of time they have available. ❑ Have an agenda if meeting. ❑ Convey bottom line and main supporting points first; keep detail ready if needed, but don't force. ❑ Distill your ideas into small number of succinct points. ❑ Have an "elevator speech" (1-minute summary of your points), along with 5- and 10-minute versions. ❑ Use diagrams/pictures that convey situation in one glance. ❑ Ensure you have a plan; don't just present problem. ❑ If leaving voice mail, plan what you'll say, keep to less than 30 seconds. ❑ Keep e-mails short/concise.

Tool 12-1. (Continued page 110)

CHECKLIST:
Matching Your Communication
to the Person Whose Help You Need

If You Know the Person ...	You Should ...
Audience Group 2 ❏ Tells stories. ❏ Engages in pleasantries. ❏ Exhibits interest in people involved in situation. ❏ Tolerates digressions. ❏ Has position that involves people issues.	❏ Speak at their pace. ❏ Make small talk first; include pleasantries in e-mail and voice mail. ❏ Ensure you have details on people involved, including effects on them. ❏ Schedule enough time to allow for off-agenda items.

Tool 12-1. (Continued)

CHECKLIST:
Matching Your Communication
to the Person Whose Help You Need

If You Know the Person ...	You Should ...
Audience Group 3 ❑ Asks for details, backup, proof. ❑ Wants to know where/how you got information. ❑ Uses spreadsheets or charts to organize/ convey information. ❑ Asks lots of questions. ❑ Has a position that involves analysis.	❑ Have detail ready; let person know immediately. ❑ Use spreadsheets, charts. ❑ Consider range of possible questions and have answers and supporting evidence ready. ❑ Ask if person wants details in advance in order to review before your meeting.

Tool 12-1. (Continued)

CHECKLIST:
Selecting the Right
Communication Medium

If You Know the Person ...	You Should ...
❏ Prefers phone/voice mail ... and uses it even when you send e-mail.	❏ Call instead of e-mailing.
❏ Prefers e-mail ... and uses it even when you leave voice mail.	❏ Send him/her e-mail instead of calling.
❏ Prefers to meet in person ... and pushes for a meeting even when you suggest a call or e-mail.	❏ Meet with him/her instead of calling/sending e-mail.

Tool 12-2.

Reality Check

A colleague of ours, Jan, was sitting in the cafeteria one day when her boss's boss's boss, Marie, sat down across from her, offered her half a muffin, and said, "I'm so glad to see you. Tell me how your Six Sigma project is going." Jan's first impulse was to whip out the data pack the team had just finished and launch into the fascinating details of their chi-square analysis. Jan loves the challenge of turning raw data into useful information, and she easily could have expounded on the team's analysis for hours.

Fortunately, Jan recalled the *Checklist: Matching Your Communication to the Person Whose Help You Need*, and recognized that going into details of the team's data analysis might not be the best approach with Marie. Although they didn't know each other well, Marie was smiling and making full eye contact. Jan quickly reviewed the times she'd seen Marie in action, and recalled that Marie was a great storyteller and really seemed to care about people. So Jan started by relating a funny story about missing the first team meeting because there was a pickle spill on the freeway. She then mentioned how excited the team was about the breakthrough they made in the last meeting, and what a developmental experience the project has been for all members. They ended up talking about the project for nearly an hour, and Marie agreed to help Jan get some much-needed data from her boss's boss.

CHAPTER 13.
How to Be a Better Listener
So That People Will Want to Help You

Good listening skills are critical to the success of your Six Sigma project. Obvious areas where listening skills come into play are in learning about the process and collecting the right data. Poor listeners won't get the right information. Less obvious—but just as critical—is the role of listening in gaining support and cooperation from your stakeholders. Specifically:

- People are more likely to cooperate when they feel you're listening to them.
- If you listen well, you'll be better able to determine whether you are really getting cooperation or just "lip service."

Becoming a better listener is not brain surgery—it's primarily a matter of knowing what to do and (more importantly) committing to making the effort. We can't help you make the commitment, but we can make some suggestions on how to improve. We recommend that you:

1. Tune in to nonverbal communication cues.*
2. Concentrate on the speaker.

*Note: The suggestions in the section on nonverbal cues apply to interactions that are face to face or via phone. While there are nonverbal cues in e-mail messages, most people are so poor at conveying information this way that interpreting their meaning is often quite difficult. See Chapter 14 for more on communicating effectively through e-mail.

Tune into Nonverbal Cues

Studies show that in conversation, we get 7% of the meaning from words and 93% from nonverbal cues. So if you're not tuned into nonverbal communication cues and what they may mean, you're missing most of what's going on!

Nonverbal cues include:

- Aspects of speech other than words: volume, tone, speed, pitch, etc.
- Gestures
- Facial expressions
- Eye movements
- Physical proximity/position
- Bodily contact

WHAT TO DO:

1. Consciously watch/listen for the speaker's nonverbal communication.
2. Be conscious of whether the overall pattern is positive or negative, and whether the speaker's words and nonverbal communications match (see Tool 13-1).
3. If the overall pattern seems negative or the speaker's nonverbal behaviors are at odds with the words used, consider whether you should act to clarify what the speaker means, test for agreement, or probe for the speaker's thoughts and feelings on the topic being discussed.

KEY PRINCIPLES:

The *overall* pattern of nonverbal cues counts more than any individual item, so don't over-interpret one cue.

Nonverbal cues mean *different things in different cultures*. The categorization of items in Tool 13-1 applies to speakers from the USA. If you're communicating with someone from another culture, you should learn all you can about nonverbal cues in that culture before trying to interpret those cues.

Concentrate on the Speaker

In a business environment in which multitasking is a way of life, concentrating all your attention on the person speaking to you may seem an impossible luxury. But if you're looking not only to gain the information you need, but also to build support and cooperation for your project, that is exactly what you need to do.

WHAT TO DO:

Follow the suggestions in Tool 13-2 for what to do before and during the conversation in order to maintain your concentration on the speaker.

CHECKLIST:
Reading Nonverbal Cues

Positive Signs	Negative Signs
Visible ❑ Frequent eye contact ❑ Leaning forward ❑ Smiling ❑ Nodding ❑ Friendly touching **Audible** ❑ Speaking in warm/friendly tone ❑ Laughing ❑ Joking (appropriately) ❑ Giving feedback to indicate interest or agreement **Note:** When a speaker's words and nonverbal communications don't match, it is often a *negative* sign. At the very least, it's an indication that you may want to probe further for the speaker's real meaning.	**Visible** ❑ Little/no eye contact ❑ Frowning or grimacing ❑ Staring impassively ❑ Rolling eyes ❑ Moving away/back ❑ Sitting far away or behind barrier ❑ Attending to other tasks ❑ Jabbing/pointing finger ❑ Turning red **Audible** ❑ Speaking louder, shouting ❑ Speaking much faster ❑ Raising vocal pitch ❑ Becoming silent or talking in monosyllables ❑ Interrupting ❑ Speaking in angry tone

Tool 13-1.

CHECKLIST:
Concentrating on the Speaker

Before the Conversation

❏ Make a conscious decision to keep an open mind, hear the person out, and not interrupt.

❏ Identify the right time and place for the conversation, and what you'll do if the speaker brings it up under other circumstances. (Will you reschedule? Have the conversation anyway?)

❏ Plan in advance for how you'll maintain your concentration during conversations in which
   - you've had unpleasant encounters with the speaker.
   - the speaker is someone who bores you.
   - the topic is one that hits one of your or the speaker's hot buttons, so the conversation could get heated.

During the Conversation

❏ Constantly monitor your concentration level and if your attention starts to wander, force yourself to refocus on the speaker. If you miss something, bite the bullet and ask the speaker to repeat or rephrase.

❏ Periodically restate the speaker's main points, ask clarifying questions, and otherwise check to ensure that you're getting the meaning of what's being said.

❏ Attend to your own nonverbal communication. Monitor your actions and voice to ensure that you're sending the right signals (i.e., those that match your words and your real feelings).

Tool 13-2. (Continued on next page)

CHECKLIST:
Concentrating on the Speaker

During the Conversation (Continued)

❑ Don't tune out because the speaker is "too emotional" or seems to be "overreacting." Commit to staying connected and continuing the conversation.

❑ Don't simultaneously do e-mail or other tasks that take your attention off the speaker.

Tool 13-2. (Continued)

Reality Check

A good example of how to use the *Checklist: Reading Nonverbal Cues* came when a Six Sigma team sponsor was giving feedback on the just-in-time Six Sigma training a Black Belt had just delivered to a project team. The sponsor had nothing but glowing things to say about the program. She stressed that the participants had been engaged and that all of them had left the program excited about getting started on the project. She praised the Black Belt's teaching skills and mentioned how rare it was to find someone good at both the technical and training aspects of Six Sigma.

Despite the positive words, however, the Black Belt noticed that the sponsor wasn't making eye contact and was leaning away with her arms crossed. She seemed to be speaking faster than normal, too. The Black Belt was puzzled, and finally asked if something might be bothering the sponsor. The sponsor grew quiet and moved a few steps away, then finally admitted that the funding had been cut for the project and she felt she had just wasted the time of the Black Belt and the participants. The two were able to have a more direct conversation after that, and made plans for deploying the recent trainees to other teams. The sponsor's relief was obvious and the two were smiling and laughing by the end of the conversation.

Had the Black Belt not noticed the "disconnect" between the sponsor's words and her nonverbal cues, he would have left the meeting on a high … only to be acutely disappointed when the lack of project funding was announced. And he would have been scrambling to figure out what to do with the recent trainees. Instead, by the time the trainees heard that their original project was off, they had already learned about their new assignments from the Black Belt. Their level of enthusiasm for Six Sigma remained high, and they were still able to make a contribution to the organization—although not on the original project. The Black Belt felt like part of a solution to the problem, rather than a victim of it.

CHAPTER 14.
How to Avoid the Pitfalls of E-Mail on Six Sigma Projects

Every interaction with others in your organization is an opportunity to either *increase* or *decrease* support for your project. If you're like the majority of Six Sigma team members, e-mail is one of the primary ways—if not the primary way—you interact with those whose support you need. So you'll want to be sure you know the pitfalls of communicating with e-mail ... and how to make sure you don't fall into them and inadvertently create resistance instead of support.

WHAT TO DO:

Use the checklist in Tool 14-1 to help you avoid the typical pitfalls of e-mail on Six Sigma projects. While it may seem cumbersome to run through this list for every e-mail you send, the goal is to make this way of thinking *automatic*. Try it a few times and soon you won't even have to look at the list ... and you'll increase the level of support and cooperation for your project.

CHECKLIST:
E-Mail Pitfalls and Avoiding Them

Pitfall	How to Avoid Pitfall
Not knowing when to use/ not use e-mail	❑ Consider alternate ways of responding, and be certain that e-mail is appropriate. ❑ Don't e-mail to avoid the recipient or his/her reaction to your message. ❑ Follow the other person's lead: if he/she usually calls or is expecting a call, then don't use e-mail. ❑ Don't "cc" people (such as someone's boss) to punish the recipient. ❑ Don't introduce an idea that might cause the recipient to resist (such as a request for resources that you know the recipient will find disturbing). ❑ Don't escalate an ongoing e-mail war. ❑ If something has upset you, take time to calm down and (if appropriate) request clarification rather than assuming the offense was intentional; refrain from firing off an e-mail in anger. ❑ If in doubt about the appropriateness of what you're sending, ask a colleague for an objective opinion on how the recipient might interpret your message.

Tool 14-1. (Continued on next page)

CHECKLIST:
E-Mail Pitfalls and Avoiding Them

Pitfall	How to Avoid Pitfall
Not taking time to establish a relationship or add a human touch	❑ Do what you can to establish a relationship with this person first, so your e-mail interactions go more smoothly. ❑ Try to meet the recipient in person or by phone if possible. ❑ Recognize that because e-mail lacks nonverbal cues, it's easy for people to misunderstand or take offense at messages. Try to reduce this possibility by ensuring that your tone is warm or at least neutral. ❑ Use "please" and "thank you." (Yes, your mother was right!) ❑ As appropriate, include positive comments on the working relationship you have with the recipient, refer to shared work experiences, exchange some personal information, etc. ❑ Include a greeting and a signature (especially when interacting with colleagues in non-U.S. countries, where there is often a higher level of formality).

Tool 14-1. (Continued)

Reality Check

Here's an example of an e-mail we saw that wasn't very effective:

I'm still waiting for your month-end figures. My deadline is Friday.

Jim, the recipient of this e-mail, did not report to Beth, the sender, nor did he know her well. So he certainly wasn't expecting to get what appeared to be a command from her. And didn't she recognize that he had his own work to do and his own deadlines? Needless to say, Jim did not immediately leap into action upon receipt of this message. Nor was his impression of Beth enhanced.

Beth, meanwhile, couldn't figure out why she didn't get a quick answer from Jim. She knew he got the e-mail, since she'd gotten the receipt. It struck her that perhaps Jim just wasn't a team player. It never occurred to Beth that perhaps her curt and seemingly demanding e-mail might have played a part in Jim's response (that is, his lack of response).

Most people think they get too much e-mail, and some argue that readers appreciate concise e-mails. That may be true, but we still think the following would have been more likely to get results for Beth:

Hi Jim,

Thanks for getting back to me so quickly with the numbers for last quarter. I'd like to include last month's figures, too, when I give my report this

*Friday. Could you possibly send me a copy of
your month-end report by Thursday? I know
you're probably in the middle of a lot of other
things, so please let me know if there's anything I
can do to help you on this.*

Thanks!

Beth

Better still, Beth might have stopped by Jim's office and
asked for a copy in person. Had Beth considered the
Checklist: E-Mail Pitfalls and Avoiding Them
before sending her message, she likely could have gotten
what she needed when she needed it.

CHAPTER 15.
How to Make an Effective Presentation About Your Six Sigma Project

As you work through your project, you will have to make a number of presentations about your progress. Your project champion might want to see whether you're following DMAIC correctly and using the right tools. The process owner may want to know how the process is performing now and what data you have to back that up. The steering committee might want to know what improvements you're considering and the risks and costs associated with each.

No matter what the audience is looking for, the bottom line is that it's not enough for you to do a good job on the project itself. You must also be able to convey information about your project in a way that gets you the outcome you're looking for—whether that be agreement to continue with the project, support for your improvement idea, credit toward certification, etc. How well you present is key to your success.

KEY PRINCIPLES:
The most important three things you can do are:

1. Follow the effective presentation techniques in the checklist (Tool 15-1).
2. Know your audience and adjust the way you speak to their style. (See Chapter 12 for details.)
3. Don't make the mistake of using Six Sigma jargon when it's not appropriate. (See explanation on page 128.)

CHECKLIST:
Effective Project Presentation

Before the Presentation

❏ Find out who will be in the audience for your presentationq
  Find out what the audience believes is the purpose of the
  presentation, and what they expect from you (information?
  justification for additional resources? savings to date?).

❏ Be clear on what you expect from the audience (approval to
  continue the project? more resources?), and present
  accordingly.

❏ Know how much time you have for the presentation.

❏ Rehearse the presentation and time it.

❏ Consider what you will do if your time is cut short, and you
  only have 5 minutes, 10 minutes, etc.

❏ Prepare an "elevator speech" of your main points.

❏ Have an appropriate number of slides for the time allowed.

❏ Build in time for Q&A.

❏ Try to identify how members of the audience like to
  communicate.

❏ Create a presentation that is appropriate (in content and
  style) for the audience.

❏ If you've been given a template, ensure your presentation
  conforms to it.

❏ If there is no template, create a presentation flow that covers
  all the high points before going into great detail.

❏ Ensure your slides are readable from a distance: good
  contrast, not too busy, large-sized font.

Tool 15-1. (Continued on next page)

CHECKLIST:
Effective Project Presentation

Before the Presentation (Continued)

❑ Ensure your slides are not filled with Six Sigma (or other) jargon that is unfamiliar to the audience.

❑ Include comprehensible pictures/diagrams, etc. that illustrate your points clearly. These should not require lengthy explanations.

❑ Have printed material available for those who need it.

❑ Check out the presentation room and make all arrangements for equipment, room set-up, etc.

❑ If you don't have a lot of experience creating presentations, get help from someone who has.

During the Presentation (read before your presentation)

❑ Face the audience, not the slides.

❑ Make appropriate eye contact.

❑ Speak clearly.

❑ Don't hide behind a podium.

❑ Look/sound alive—show some passion for the topic.

❑ Be attentive to audience reactions. Watch for signs that they want you to move on or that they don't understand you.

❑ For an audience not steeped in Six Sigma jargon, minimize the use of the terms and explain the terms you do use.

❑ Refer to notes if you must, but don't read from a script.

❑ Don't read the slides to the audience.

❑ Keep track of time and know how much you have left.

Tool 15-1. (Continued)

What Do You Mean, I Shouldn't Use Six Sigma Jargon?

One of the goals in Six Sigma is to get everyone speaking the same language, i.e., the language of Six Sigma. So you should set an example by using it as much as possible, right?

Six Sigma professionals often make a mistake in this area that results in their getting *less* rather than *more* support and cooperation for their projects.

While speaking the language of Six Sigma is an admirable corporate goal, the way this is actually implemented is of paramount importance. If you want to get support and cooperation, you have to start by meeting people on their *own* ground and speaking to them in their *own* language. Once you have their attention and trust, you can gradually introduce new language—providing you do so in a way that is instructive, not condescending. If you make people feel as if they are stupid or not part of the "elite," then they will not be inclined to support you or your project. This is particularly the case when you're communicating with people who have familiarity with other quality initiatives, but not with Six Sigma.

So speak in your stakeholders' language, and introduce them to "Six Sigma speak" slowly and tactfully. You'll get much more buy-in this way.

Reality Check

We worked with a Six Sigma team on a project involving large-scale change across a complex organization. The team needed to make a presentation to the CEO, who did not have a detailed view of that organization. The team leader had a 60-slide PowerPoint presentation, but the ***Checklist: Effective Project Presentation*** helped her realize that she would have to capture his attention in the first five minutes or he would be lost … and would likely tune out or (worse) end the meeting.

We knew that the CEO was a visual thinker; whenever he spoke, it was always with a flipchart at hand, and he'd draw diagrams to illustrate his points. So we advised the team leader to keep the wordy slides in her "back pocket." We helped her design a giant poster, with figures representing the various parts of the organization, the current interrelationships among them, and the probable changes that the project would create in those interrelationships. While the poster included a few words, the information was primarily visual.

At the presentation, the team leader spent a few minutes orienting the CEO to the poster and what it depicted. She then let the CEO direct the discussion. The presentation moved at the CEO's pace, in the order of his choosing, and at a depth that he dictated. The PowerPoint slides never made it out of the team leader's back pocket. The CEO did not leave the meeting with in-depth knowledge of what the team had been working on. He *did* leave with a global view of where the organization had been and was going … and the team leader left with his full support for the project.

CHAPTER 16.
What to Do When You're Not Getting Cooperation

The success of your Six Sigma project depends in good part on cooperation from people on your team and across the larger organization. So what do you do when you can't get cooperation, when people resist?

Let us be very clear: the best way to deal with resistance is to prevent it, which means planning in advance (see Chapter 10). But not all resistance can be prevented, so when you do encounter what you think is resistance, take this general approach:

1. Learn to recognize whether what's happening really is resistance (see checklist in Tool 16-1).
2. Understand possible reasons why people would resist your project (see Tool 16-2).
3. Learn and apply steps to minimizing the resistance (see Tool 16-3).

CHECKLIST:
Recognizing Resistance to Your Six Sigma Project

❑ **Compliance**

Description:
Immediate agreement: no reservations, concerns, or questions. Or the person treats you like a savior.

Words you may hear:
I don't need to know anything more—let's just do the project. I'll bet you'll work miracles here!

❑ **Avoidance**

Description:
Lip service to your request, but no follow-up action. Claim that the problem is already solved or can't be. Silence or one-word answers.

Words you may hear:
I'd love to help but it's too hectic. We've tried all that quality stuff, but it didn't work. This place is different.

❑ **Flooding**

Description:
Overwhelming detail, much of it irrelevant to the issue. You can't make sense of it all.

Words you may hear:
Well, it all started 10 years ago. We have 15 years of reports. Sorry they aren't in any order....

Tool 16-1. (Continued on next page)

CHECKLIST:
Recognizing Resistance to
Your Six Sigma Project

❏ **Intellectualizing**

Description:
Theoretical discussions when you need action.

Words you may hear:
So, I'm just fascinated by DOE—can you show me how it works?

❏ **Attacking**

Description:
Questions about your competence, qualifications, experience, etc. Sometimes: confrontation, anger, finger-pointing, competing, etc.

Words you may hear:
So what do you really know? Look, I've been using these quality tools since you were in high school.

❏ **Refusal**

Description:
The stakeholder may refuse point-blank to work with you.

Words you may hear:
I don't have time for this! Some of us have real work to do.

Tool 16-1. (Continued)

Why Might People Not Cooperate with Your Project?

People may be uncooperative or resistant for variety of reasons. Some of these reasons might seem understandable to you, while others may strike you as unsupportable or even petty. We recommend that you refrain from making value judgments about the reasons. Instead, you should to try to discern the possible underlying causes for the resistance and deal with it as best you can. Use Tool 16-2 for identifying causes of uncooperative behavior.

CHECKLIST:
Identifying Reasons People May Resist Your Six Sigma Project

Have you considered these possible reasons for resistance?

❑ Satisfaction with the current situation; lack of need to change (process works fine, or current methods will fix any problems).

❑ Belief that Six Sigma is a poor solution to the organization's problems.

❑ Concern with resources and time required for Six Sigma.

❑ Fear of being viewed as incompetent as result of data being collected.

❑ Lack of information or understanding about what's going on.

❑ Perception that there's nothing in it for them.

❑ Fear of statistics.

❑ Fear of loss of power or status due to organization changes, process focus, etc.

❑ Concern with no longer being the "expert" ... especially if this is an ex-quality person not trained in Six Sigma.

❑ Mistrust or animosity based on experience with previous quality programs.

❑ Change overload due to too many organizational initiatives or no sense of how they all connect.

❑ Inertia, habit.

❑ Sense of being overwhelmed with work and having no time to deal with Six Sigma too.

Tool 16-2. (Continued on next page)

CHECKLIST:
Identifying Reasons People May Resist Your Six Sigma Project

Have you considered these possible reasons for resistance?

❑ Perception that Six Sigma will take the fun/creativity/heart out of work.

❑ Discomfort with implying that previous management didn't do a good job with the process.

Tool 16-2. (Continued)

Example of Resistance and Its Underlying Reason

RESISTANCE BEHAVIOR

During root-cause analysis, a process owner disputes the validity of the data, claiming that you collected the wrong information because you don't know what you're doing (attacking) or that it was an unusual month so the data is meaningless (avoiding).

A POSSIBLE REASON FOR THE BEHAVIOR

The root cause is something the process owner now realizes he should have addressed long ago, and he fears that acknowledging it now might make him appear incompetent. Since he cannot admit this, he instead attacks you or looks for ways to avoid the issue.

A WARNING

If you really don't know what you're doing or the data really is from a nonrepresentative month, then this may be common sense rather than resistance!

WHAT TO DO WHEN STAKEHOLDERS RESIST YOUR PROJECT ... AND WHAT NOT TO DO

Tool 16-3 provides guidance on how to effectively deal with resistance behavior ... and what not to do.

CHECKLIST:
Do's and Don'ts for Dealing with
Resistance to Your Six Sigma Project

Do ...

- ❑ Start by giving the "resistor" the benefit of the doubt. Consider whether he/she is truly resisting your good idea, or just reacting sensibly to a poor idea.

- ❑ Take what you've learned from this chapter's checklist on reasons for resistance and fill out the Checklist: Project Stakeholder Analysis in Chapter 10.

- ❑ Use the Worksheet: Project Stakeholder Planning (Tool 10-5) in Chapter 10 to create a small plan for addressing this person's specific reason for resistance and gaining his/her cooperation.

- ❑ Be sensitive and tactful when presenting data that might threaten this person (such as root cause or performance data).

- ❑ Exhibit patience, respect, and empathy.

- ❑ Stay connected. Don't be put off by the person's emotion.

- ❑ Maintain focus and perspective, and relax. Use the Chapter 10 worksheets to methodically work your way through this problem one step at a time, just as you do when you apply the DMAIC approach.

- ❑ Review the suggestions for how to prevent resistance (see Chapter 10). If you haven't been following these suggestions start doing so now.

Tool 16-3. (Continued on next page)

CHECKLIST:
Do's and Don'ts for Dealing with
Resistance to Your Six Sigma Project

Don't ...

❑ Force or manipulate people into compliance.
❑ Use persuasion when it's not appropriate (see Chapter 11).
❑ Continue as if everything is just fine.
❑ Assume you can't do anything and just give up.
❑ Lie.

Adapted from Rick Maurer's *Beyond the Wall of Resistance*

Tool 16-3. (Continued)

Reality Check

Todd was leading a Six Sigma project that seemed to have come to a halt in the Measure phase. Joe, the team member responsible for gathering data from Jane, the department manager, just couldn't seem to get what he needed from her. He'd tried various approaches, using e-mail reminders, voice mail messages, attempts at face-to-face meetings. Nothing worked. The manager made promises … weeks passed … still no data. At this rate, Todd thought, the project could take a year or more!

Then another team member, Sylvia, suggested that they stop bemoaning the lack of data and instead apply Six Sigma principles to the problem. "We say we've tried everything," she said to the team, "but don't we need to know the root cause of this problem before we identify the solution?" Somewhat embarrassed at not having thought of this himself, Todd suggested that the team devote a meeting to analyzing the problem in detail.

The team's first question: were they seeing resistance or just good intentions gone awry? Using the ***Checklist: Recognizing Resistance to Your Six Sigma Project***, the team saw two kinds of behavior that fit their situation. When Joe first spoke to Jane about what data the team would need, he barely got the words out before she said, "Hey, no problem! Anything you need—just ask and it's yours. I know you Belts will be able to fix all our problems." Oddly, she hadn't asked Joe a single question—not even what he planned to do with the data. But when Joe followed up with a detailed list of what he wanted, some-how Jane could just never get around to it. Nor was she available for calls or meetings. This sounded very much like *compliance* followed by *avoidance*. The team con-cluded that they were indeed up against resistance.

Next, the team consulted the ***Checklist: Identifying Reasons People May Resist Your Six Sigma Project*** to help them figure out why Jane might be resisting. The item about fear of being viewed as incompetent jumped out at them, as did the one on concerns about not being the "expert." They recalled that Jane had been part of the com-pany's TQM effort five years earlier. In fact, she'd been trained in many of the same tools they were using in Six Sigma, yet she hadn't been trained as a Black Belt or Green Belt. When the TQM initiative fell apart, Jane ended up in a line job. Todd recalled hearing that she wanted to get out of that job and had been hurt and annoyed about being passed over for a Belt position, as she much preferred that kind of role. Joe recalled Jane's remark about "you Belts" fixing all her department's problems. In retrospect, this sounded less like a show of faith and more like resent-ment—with a bit of fear underneath. After all, shouldn't a department run by a former quality expert have solved its own quality problems already?

Armed with this new perspective on the situation with Jane, Todd and the team were able to create a "stakehold-er plan" that incorporated a targeted influence strategy and set of tactics. Finally they began to make some progress on getting the latest data.

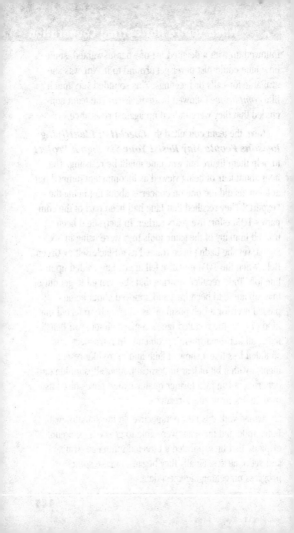

CHAPTER 17.
Sample Plans for Getting Buy-in

THE SCENARIO:

Jasmine Doe is the CEO of a mid-sized company that manufactures state-of-the-art components for the video editing industry. The company has had a Six Sigma program for just over a year, and the team that worked on the New Product to Market project was wildly successful, even getting some press for their efforts.

With the significant reduction in the time it took to develop the last new product, it became obvious that the new product marketing cycle couldn't keep up. There is a lot of energy in the company to launch a new Six Sigma team to improve the marketing process.

Even with less than adequate marketing, the new product is selling better than expected. Jasmine has been doing a great deal of personal promotion with customers. Discus-sions keep getting sidetracked, however, by complaints about the company's billing system. Invoices arrive late, are hard to understand, and have errors, and no one at the home office seems to have any answers when the customers complain. Jasmine has decided to launch a Six Sigma team to improve the billing process before or maybe at the same time as the marketing improvement process. She's not really sure the billing project is worth the effort of a Six Sigma team, but she's had it with listening to complaints.

Jasmine called a meeting with Art Lee, the manager of the billing department, and William Boyd, VP of MIS. Art agreed that the project would be a good idea, mainly because it would make the clerks in his department happy to be on a Six Sigma project. He was, however, a bit annoyed that it took so long to get Six Sigma resources for his department. He even went so far as to imply that Jasmine helped cause the billing problem by withholding resources in spite of his repeated requests. Things got a little tense at this point of the meeting.

Bill Boyd said he thought the marketing project was a lot more important to the company. (Jasmine secretly agrees, as this is where her interests and skills lie, but part of her recognizes the need to deal with the invoicing issues.) And he felt a bit defensive, since he helped create the original billing process. But Bill reluctantly agreed to let the majority rule, as long as nobody tried to tell him how to run MIS (like that Black Belt working on the new product development cycle did last year).

As a result of the discussion at the meeting, Jasmine has assigned a Black Belt, Thomas, to the Billing Improvement project. Following are sample plans for getting buy-in on a Six Sigma project to improve billing processes. We've included a plan for Thomas and the project team to use to:

- Get buy-in from senior management (J. Doe, CEO)
- Get buy-in from middle management (W. Boyd, MIS VP)
- Get buy-in from line workers (Billing Department clerks)

SAMPLE PROJECT STAKEHOLDER
IDENTIFICATION WORKSHEET WITH MAP

Names/Titles	Map
T. Ray: Mktg VP	
M. Brown: HR VP	
R. Jones: Ops VP	
W. Boyd: MIS VP	
B. Smith: MIS Mgr	
J. Doe: CEO	
A. Lee: Billing Mgr	
Billing Dept Clerks	
MIS Contractors	

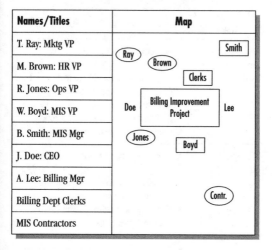

SAMPLE SENIOR MANAGEMENT
STAKEHOLDER ANALYSIS

Name of Stakeholder:	Jasmine Doe/CEO
What I need from this stakeholder	<ul><li>Get her to assign resources to this project.</li><li>Get her to support/talk positively about this project so people want to help.</li><li>Make her have a good opinion of me as a Six Sigma professional so I get good reviews and future assignments.</li></ul>
Stakeholder's interests	<ul><li>To improve customer satisfaction with billing</li><li>To free up resources to work on the marketing process project</li><li>To get the most return possible from each Six Sigma project</li><li>To retain employees</li><li>To build enthusiasm for Six Sigma in the company</li><li>To reduce cost, of course, since there's constant pressure to do so</li></ul>

Tool 17-1. (Continued on pages 151-153)

SAMPLE SENIOR MANAGEMENT
STAKEHOLDER ANALYSIS

Name of Stakeholder:	Jasmine Doe/CEO
How stakeholder may benefit from my project	• Customer complaints about billing could be reduced, and Jasmine can get back to marketing the new product without customers turning the conversation to billing problems. • Resources will be freed up to work on the marketing process. • The billing department has a turnover rate twice that in other departments, at least partly due to frustration with poor processes. • A big and visible success would help build enthusiasm for Six Sigma. • It could reduce costs.
How stakeholder may be hurt / inconvenienced by my project	• Resources are tight. To free them up for me, she's had to postpone the marketing process project and may have to take people off other projects. • Improving the billing process isn't as exciting as some other Six Sigma projects (i.e., the one for the marketing process) that could use the resources.

Tool 17-1. (Continued)

SAMPLE SENIOR MANAGEMENT
STAKEHOLDER ANALYSIS

Name of Stakeholder:	Jasmine Doe/CEO
Probable response from stakeholder. If resistance, why?	• Don't know. She's been on the fence. I know she picked this project over one for the marketing process, but heard that it was done reluctantly.
How big a gap between what I need and probable response?	• Probably some gap. She knows the billing processes need to be overhauled, but may not be willing to be as vocal with her support as I need her to be.
Key influence "levers"	• Customer dissatisfaction with the performance of the current billing processes, and how that has distracted them from the new product. • My good reputation for getting things done. • The need to reduce turnover in the billing department. • Cost reduction.

Tool 17-1. (Continued)

SAMPLE SENIOR MANAGEMENT STAKEHOLDER ANALYSIS

Name of Stakeholder:	Jasmine Doe/CEO
Stakeholder's communications needs	• Jasmine is a "people person." She likes to hear the story behind the results. She listens to her voice-mail, but seldom checks e-mail.
Details/history of any conflicts with stakeholder (including conflict on the project team)	• Things got a little heated in the meeting where this project was proposed. The head of billing (Art Lee) was somewhat insulting when he suggested that Jasmine had already created a customer problem by not funding a process improvements earlier.
Other relevant info about this stakeholder or situation	• Her contract is up for renewal. Jasmine has promised the Board that the new product will be a blockbuster, and customer complaints about invoicing could get in the way of her being able to deliver on that promise.

Tool 17-1. (Continued)

SAMPLE SENIOR MANAGEMENT STAKEHOLDER PLAN

Name of Stakeholder:	Jasmine Doe/CEO
Specific influence objective	• Have her tell Art Lee to give me Linda as a full-time team member, and another two people part-time. • Get her to highlight this project in her senior team meeting next week, and to work on getting Bill Smith on board. • Put me on the marketing project when I'm done with this.
How to increase (or reframe) benefits to this stakeholder	• Quantify the potential benefits of this project, including reduced customer complaints, reduced turnover in billing, and reduced costs. • Emphasize that this project, while not as exciting as some others, will a) let her focus clients on the new product without the distraction of billing problems, and b) be a guaranteed win that will be visible to the company.

Tool 17-2. (Continued on pages 155-156)

SAMPLE SENIOR MANAGEMENT STAKEHOLDER PLAN

Name of Stakeholder:	Jasmine Doe/CEO
How to deal with a conflict with this stakeholder	• Avoid confrontations between Jasmine and Art. • Focus on the benefits of the improved processes, rather than the embarrassment of our current ones.
Plan for direct influence	• Quantify the benefits, especially in cost savings. Give her the data she needs to impress the Board. • Offer my help on the marketing project next quarter if she will support this project now.
Plan for indirect influence	• Ask R. Jones to talk to her about the great project we did together last year. • Ask billing clerks to let her know how much better this project will make their jobs.

Tool 17-2. (Continued)

SAMPLE SENIOR MANAGEMENT
STAKEHOLDER PLAN

Name of Stakeholder:	Jasmine Doe/CEO
Implementation considerations (including timing and communications approach)	• Make sure the project is complete before her contract is reviewed. • Take advantage of her office being on the same floor to chat about the project informally.

Tool 17-2. (Continued)

SAMPLE MIDDLE MANAGEMENT STAKEHOLDER ANALYSIS

Name of Stakeholder:	William Boyd/VP of MIS
What I need from this stakeholder	• Get his agreement to assign resources to this billing process improvement project. • Need him to talk this project up to the CEO.
Stakeholder's interests	• To look competent and in control— if there are going to be changes, he wants to be in the driver's seat. • To retain his people. • To look good to the CEO ... wants to show he "adds value." • To work on the newest technology and most visible projects. • To reduce cost, of course, since there's constant pressure to do so.

Tool 17-3. (Continued on pages 158-161)

Name of Stakeholder:	William Boyd/VP of MIS
How stakeholder may benefit from my project	• If the process is improved, his department won't be dealing with all the repetitive requests for changes and reports that they're getting now. • Since he's short on people because of the hiring freeze, anything that would free up some of his people would benefit him. He'd put them on the new marketing project, which is highly visible (good for him politically) and involves new technology (good for his people, who are bored with maintaining the billing system and are starting to send out their resumes). • Could reduce costs.
How stakeholder may be hurt/ inconvenienced by my project	• He could lose face. He created the original system and set up the billing process as it exists today, so anything that implies that he didn't do a good job is going to make him unhappy.

Tool 17-3. (Continued)

SAMPLE MIDDLE MANAGEMENT STAKEHOLDER ANALYSIS

Name of Stakeholder:	William Boyd/VP of MIS
How stakeholder may be hurt/ inconvenienced by my project	• He's going to have to put even more people on the billing system for the short term—maybe the next six months— before he can reallocate to the new marketing system. That's not going to make them happy—six months seems like an eternity to those 20-somethings on his staff.
Probable response from stakeholder. If resistance, why?	• Likely to be resistant to the idea that there's something wrong with the billing process he helped create. • Won't be happy about allocating any more resources to the supporting system than he absolutely has to. • Might mention to the CEO what he already said to R. Jones: that we'd be better off doing a project in the HR department, where it takes them three months to make an address change. And the CEO is already on the fence....

Tool 17-3. (Continued)

SAMPLE MIDDLE MANAGEMENT STAKEHOLDER ANALYSIS

Name of Stakeholder:	William Boyd/VP of MIS
How big a gap between what I need and probable response?	• Looks big ... I need him to commit wholeheartedly, and it doesn't look as if he is going to have a great reaction ... at least at first.
Key influence "levers"	• Boyd's interest in getting involved in the marketing system. • Boyd's desire to get more clout with the CEO. • The interest of Boyd's employees in working on a better system and not dealing with the endless billing questions/problems any more. • Cost reduction.

Tool 17-3. (Continued)

SAMPLE MIDDLE MANAGEMENT STAKEHOLDER ANALYSIS

Name of Stakeholder:	William Boyd/VP of MIS
Stakeholder's communications needs	• He's a guy who wants a lot of detail—the more Excel spreadsheets, the better. He's always asking for data, wants to know exactly where you got it, has no interest in opinions from non-experts, likes to see a well-laid out plan for everything. Definitely an e-mail guy too—I think he likes to see the exact words in front of him so he can pick the ideas apart!
Details/history of any conflicts with stakeholder (including conflict on the project team)	• Had a bad experience last year with a Black Belt that came to work on a project in MIS—said the guy was a know-it-all.
Other relevant info about this stakeholder or situation	• For all his data orientation, he really cares about his people—spends a lot of time thinking about how to retain them.

Tool 17-3. (Continued)

SAMPLE MIDDLE MANAGEMENT
STAKEHOLDER PLAN

Name of Stakeholder:	William Boyd/VP of MIS
Specific influence objective	• I need him to give me two people to help me gather data and do some testing—figure 20% of their time for the next two months. • Need him to speak positively about this to the CEO, who's on the fence re the worth of the project.
How to increase (or reframe) benefits to this stakeholder	• Help him to recognize that this will help free up people for work on the marketing system. • Point out freeing up his people to work on the marketing system will help him retain employees. • Get the VP of Marketing to include him in developing the marketing system. • Demonstrate the potential cost reduction.
How to reduce (or reframe) "cost" or inconvenience to this stakeholder	• Involve him up front in problem/solution definition so he doesn't lose face. • Ensure his people are excited about fixing problems and being freed up for new project.

Tool 17-4. (Continued pages 163-164)

Name of Stakeholder:	William Boyd/VP of MIS
How to deal with a conflict with this stakeholder	• Avoid discussions of that Black Belt from last year • Make sure he can see that I understand what's important to him.
Plan for direct influence	• Meet with him to get him involved at the early stages of the project so that he can help frame it and minimize loss of face • Give him say-so in resource allocation • Work with him to determine how best to reduce costs.
Plan for indirect influence	• Ask R. Jones (Ops VP) to talk to him about the project I did in Ops ... tell him that I know what I'm doing, I'll get him involved, the improvement potential and cost savings can be great. Make sure Jones doesn't present me as a "know-it-all."

Tool 17-4. (Continued)

SAMPLE MIDDLE MANAGEMENT
STAKEHOLDER PLAN

Name of Stakeholder:	William Boyd/VP of MIS
Plan for indirect influence	• Ask Ray, Marketing VP, to get Boyd involved in new Marketing now, and talk to his people to get them fired up. • Speak to some of Boyd's people myself— the ones I'm friends with—re the need for a little more of their time now so that they'll be getting fewer requests re the billing system.
Implementation considerations (including timing and communications approach)	• Talk to Boyd after R. Jones and Ray have a chance to talk to him. • Don't talk to Boyd's people until after I talk to him, as he might see that as going behind his back.

Tool 17-4. (Continued)

SAMPLE LINE WORKER
STAKEHOLDER ANALYSIS

Name of Stakeholder:	Billing Clerks
What I need from this stakeholder	• Willing volunteers to work on the team. • Others to backfill for the team members. • Enthusiasm for the project.
Stakeholder's interests	• To decrease the percentage of time they spend handling complaints and work-arounds because of a bad process. • To stop losing people (who aren't always replaced). • To look good to senior management. • To reduce their needlessly huge workload.
How stakeholder may benefit from my project	• Less boring work. • Visibility to senior management. • Less work—can get home at a decent time.

Tool 17-5. (Continued on pages 166-168)

SAMPLE LINE WORKER
STAKEHOLDER ANALYSIS

Name of Stakeholder:	Billing Clerks
How stakeholder may be hurt/ inconvenienced by my project	• Could lose face if problems with current process are perceived to be their fault. • Greater workload in the short term, while the team is working.
Probable response from stakeholder. If resistance, why?	• Likely to be excited, if they are on the team. • Might be resistant to picking up the slack with day-to-day work.
How big a gap between what I need and probable response?	• Not very big, but need to address short-term workload issues, even if they aren't raised in an open forum.

Tool 17-5. (Continued)

SAMPLE LINE WORKER
STAKEHOLDER ANALYSIS

Name of Stakeholder:	Billing Clerks
Key influence "levers"	• Reduction in customer complaints they'll have to handle. • Reduction in their workload. • Interest in being perceived as valuable to the organization. • Addition of valuable skills to their resumes.
Stakeholder's communications needs	• Who ever communicates with these folks? The more they know, in as many different forms as possible, the better. Especially the ones not on the team. They really want to be involved.
Details/history of any conflicts with stakeholder (including conflict on the project team)	• There has been some in-fighting in the department. Linda Connor really wants to be on the team, and thinks she should be chosen because she's been here the longest.

Tool 17-5. (Continued)

SAMPLE LINE WORKER
STAKEHOLDER ANALYSIS

Name of Stakeholder:	Billing Clerks
Other relevant info about this stakeholder or situation	• The department is down two FTE. With the hiring freeze, it's unlikely that they will be replaced.

Tool 17-5. (Continued)

SAMPLE LINE WORKER
STAKEHOLDER PLAN

Name of Stakeholder:	Billing Clerks
Specific influence objective	• Get Linda and two others to work on the team. • Get the others to backfill for the team members. • When they're in the cafeteria with their co-workers, want them to talk positively about the project so that Six Sigma starts to get a good grassroots reputation.
How to increase (or reframe) benefits to this stakeholder	• Show them the project will decrease the percentage of time they spend handling complaints. • Get them in front of senior management when it comes time to present the project. • Have them talk to the clerks in HR about how their workload dropped after we did a DMAIC project on the benefit enrollment process.

Tool 17-6. (Continued on pages 170-171)

SAMPLE LINE WORKER
STAKEHOLDER PLAN

Name of Stakeholder:	Billing Clerks
How to reduce (or reframe) "cost" or inconvenience to this stakeholder	• Point out that a short-term increase in workload will lead to a long-term decrease. • Assure those not on the team that there will be a forum for getting their input.
How to deal with a conflict with this stakeholder	• Talk directly to Art about allowing Linda to be on the team ... see what kind of a "trade" we can make.
Plan for direct influence	• Meet with clerks to outline the plans in detail. • Ask for their involvement, and develop a schedule for roundtable meetings with all of them. • Point out that the extra work they have to do now will pay off in the future and when it comes to promotions and performance reviews.

Tool 17-6. (Continued)

SAMPLE LINE WORKER
STAKEHOLDER PLAN

Name of Stakeholder:	Billing Clerks
Plan for indirect influence	• Everyone listens to Linda. It's crucial to get her on board. • Talk to Art about including Six Sigma project goals in everyone's objectives for the year. • Ask Jasmine to stop by and ask how the project is going.
Implementation considerations (including timing and communications approach)	• Get the issue of Linda's membership on the team settled first. • Schedule monthly updates with entire department.

Tool 17-6. (Continued)

CONCLUSION
Final Thoughts on Using This Pocket Guide

We expect that readers of this *Pocket Guide* will have one of two reactions to these tools and approaches:

1. This is exactly what I need to make my Six Sigma projects a success!
2. Am I going to be able to do this? And even if I *can*, do I *have to*? I got involved in Six Sigma because I enjoy using my analytical ability. Can't everyone just be logical and rational so we can get these projects done?

While we hope that you've had the first reaction, we recognize why you might have the second. So to anyone with those concerns, we respond:

1. Yes, you can do this. While using the tools may not come naturally at first, neither do many other things that later become second nature. (Think of learning to drive.) And you'll have the *Pocket Guide* to fall back on.
2. No, you don't have to ... but you may want to, for two reasons:
   - You can't force or "logic" people into supporting your project. Though force may sometimes appear to work, it's generally not an effective approach ... nor does this enhance your reputation in the organization. Further, when people consider whether they will support you, they do not rely on logic alone (sometimes they don't rely on it at all!).

- Practicing the approaches described in this book can help your career. People with both technical and team/influence skills are much more promotable and marketable than those with only one or the other.

So what should you do now?

PROJECT TEAM LEADERS:

- Introduce your team members to the *Pocket Guide* and its concepts, and encourage them to get familiar with the approaches and tools.
- Tell the team you're committed to following the guide as the team does its project work.
- Invite the team to work together on stakeholder identification, analysis, and planning. Not only will this result in a better plan (since it will be based on the knowledge of several people), but it also gets the team working together.
- If your company selects and/or promotes Black Belts at least partly on the basis of suitability for future leadership positions, let your manager know about your new team and influence skills.
- Introduce the *Pocket Guide* concepts to whoever is responsible for Master Black Belt, Black Belt, and Green Belt development. The more people who use the guide's tools and approaches on their projects, the better for the overall Six Sigma initiative.

PROJECT TEAM MEMBERS:

- If your project team leader introduces the *Pocket*

Guide to the team, cooperate in following the
approaches and tools.

- If your team leader doesn't have the *Pocket Guide*,
introduce him/her to it, and suggest that the team start
using the approach and tools. Do this one on one
(*not* in front of the team), and prior to the first team
meeting if possible. You might want to show the team
leader the chapters on preparing for and running the
first team meeting.

- Even if the team doesn't adopt the *Pocket Guide*, use
the tools on your own piece of the project work.

ALL:

- Think about previous Six Sigma (or other) projects
you've worked on. Identify ways the project might have
gone more smoothly or where it might have run into
trouble. Think of what might have been the root
cause(s) of any nontechnical problems you encoun-
tered during that project. Consider whether and how
you could have benefited from using the approaches
and tools outlined in this guide.

- Think about your current project and how it's progress-
ing. Identify which of the tools in the *Pocket Guide* you
could use right now to make the project go more
smoothly.

- If you're interested in attending a workshop that
teaches these techniques in detail, contact Rath &
Strong.

This guide is designed to increase your ability to get your

Six Sigma projects completed successfully. Whether you're leading the project team, participating part-time, or providing subject matter expertise when needed, the tools in the *Pocket Guide* can help you contribute to the project's success.

We hope you've found it useful.